Celebrate Change

Embracing Life's Changing Seasons

Celebrate Change

Embracing Life's Changing Seasons

Dr. Wanda A. Turner

Treasure House

An Imprint of
Destiny Image® Publishers, Inc.
P.O. Box 310
Shippensburg, PA 17257-0310

"For where your treasure is, there will your heart be also."
Matthew 6:21

ISBN 0-7684-3031-3

For Worldwide Distribution
Printed in the U.S.A.

This book and all other Destiny Image, Revival Press, MercyPlace, Fresh Bread, Destiny Image Fiction, and Treasure House books are available at Christian bookstores and distributors worldwide.

For a U.S. bookstore nearest you, call **1-800-722-6774**.
For more information on foreign distributors, call **717-532-3040**.
Or reach us on the Internet: **www.reapernet.com**

Dedication

This book is dedicated to my husband,
Andrew Carnegie Turner, II
the awesome instrument
in the hand of God
authorized to usher me into *celebrating change*!

Acknowledgments

I wish to take this opportunity to thank
the Lord Jesus Christ
and all the wonderful people He placed
in my life to make
this book happen!
Special regards to Michelle Jones, Dr. Ronn Elmore,
and all my special friends who
walked with me during this season of life.
They include:
Dr. Phyllis Carter,
D'etta West,
D. Marilyn Fullard,
Dr. Leona Weeks,
Dr. Judy Brown,
Dr. Donald Wright,
and Dr. Mary Sims.

Thanks also to Don Nori, Don Milam, and all the Destiny Image family!

Contents

"Once upon a time there was a woman named Wanda Ann who lived in California..."

Change

Chapter One

An Invitation to Change

Therefore if any man be in Christ, he is a new creature: old things are passed away; behold, all things are become new.

—2 Corinthians 5:17

"He who rejects change is the architect of decay. The only human institution which rejects progress is the cemetery."

—Harold Wilson

Oh my God. Am I really sitting here at the funeral of my husband, my friend, my lover, my pastor, my bishop? Is this real? Surely any minute now someone will shake me and mercifully rouse me from this horror.

But no one rescued me. The screams that seemed so loud to my own ears went unheard. I continued walking down that long center aisle of the First Church of God in Inglewood, California, the same city where my husband, Wayne Sylvester Davis, had preached, prayed, and pastored for so many years.

Hundreds of people—friends, family, and others—flashed by me as I moved, like frames of an old movie. I didn't recognize faces. I couldn't

3

remember names, only expressions. Sympathetic. Sorry. Tender. Curious. Bored. Stricken. *Was that a smile?* Concerned. Overwhelmed. Images were discernible but disjointed. Hands reaching out to touch me. A limousine. A sign. *Forest Lawn Cemetery*. Prayers, songs, and crying. *So much crying*. A folded United States flag. Then silence as the reality of death draped its smothering shroud over us all.

The funeral was an event to many—an occurrence that was not without pain or the ordeal of mourning, but an event just the same. It had a beginning, a middle, and an end. It could be put on a Day Planner or talked about as something that had "happened." It was a climax to the grief of many. For those of us who lived with and loved Wayne, however, the funeral was merely a portal to an ordained season of desolation, emptiness, struggle, isolation, and anguish. For me it was also a season of dark wandering and wondering.

Lord, my precious children Wendy and Steven, Whitney and Timothy, and my new grandson, Steven Wayne. What will we do? For so long that question had a ready answer. "What will we do?" was always met confidently with "We'll ask Wayne" or "Let's ask Daddy." It was like the floor beneath me. It was there, no matter where I went: that certainty that Wayne could fix things, move things, remove things, or handle things. Ask Wayne. My God, he was no longer around to give advice, bestow wise counsel, or offer protection. The man I had loved, respected, served, and shared my entire life with was now resting in the arms of Jesus. *Oh Jesus, what shall I do?*

Somehow, I had heard Him whisper to me that this day was coming. But in my flesh, in my denial, I had ignored the voice. I was insistent. I kept believing that God was going to heal Wayne Davis and raise him up as a witness that "nothing is too hard for God." Instead, He chose to set my husband free from sickness and pain, then snatch Wayne quickly to Himself. He would become one of the many "dead in Christ." I did not want him to suffer, so the grace of his end was not lost on me. But most of what was familiar to me went with him, and my soul fought for bearings.

4

I had two daughters beginning new lives with their new husbands. And there was First Apostolic Church of Inglewood. Many in the congregation of Wayne's church never knew how ill he was and didn't have the opportunity to say good-bye. They were angry and hurt. And they needed someone to blame. I knew in my mind that "hurt people hurt people," but I was unprepared for the force of their animosity. And in my own pain, I found release in reaction. The wounds of our hearts became the weapons of warfare.

I begged God for strength to handle gossip, betrayal, defection, and malicious assaults on my character. I pleaded with Him to give us understanding and compassionate hearts. I needed His mercy moving through the people at New Bethel so they could see past my quick words, rash decisions, and short temper. In my pain and sorrow, I had hurt so many of them.

Then there was World Won For Christ Ministries International, a collection of churches, missions, pastors, and bishops that faithfully served under the headship of Bishop Davis. They were in shock. What would I do about them and the vision God had entrusted to them? Who would lead them now?

All these cares piled themselves on my already heavy heart and mind. Peace was a hard-fought-for commodity. Rest took its leave of me often. And joy. Joy? It was at best elusive and more often than not chose to give me over to quiet withdrawal. And, as if the gifts of peace, rest, and joy were not already unreachable enough, I had to contend with the bitterness and anger of my late husband's family. Wayne had left behind parents and six brothers and three sisters. His death should have been a time for us to bond in our commonality. We should have been able to share our hurts and pains as well as find comfort in the memory of a man who played such a dominant role in all our lives.

But Wayne's death separated us. My daughters needed their uncles and aunts; I needed as many connections to Wayne as possible. And yet, except for Warner and Helen (*bless their hearts*), no one reached for us.

No one seemed to be able to say, "We love you. We're here for you. Thank you for taking care of our brother, our son."

It was a difficult season. It was as if satan had deliberately stirred up every serene and settled circumstance of my life and God was commanding me to navigate the turbid waters using faith as my vessel, oar, and compass. So I rowed, with great difficulty at first. I sometimes lost my focus when I considered the unfairness or the uncertainty of my situation. At times my own sorrow robbed me of peace, and fear and loneliness threatened to overtake me.

But in our seasons of greatest peril, God shows up with the most miraculous provision. What a wonderful time it was for my family and close friends to step up and say, "Hey, we're here for you"; "Turn left here, not right"; "Let me take this load from you"; or "I've prayed you through this hard patch."

My mother, my father, my brothers and sisters, listened to my cries of stress, pain, and anger. So many times they dropped everything to come to my rescue. When I couldn't go any further, there were friends and brothers and sisters in Christ from the east, west, north, and south who came to see about me and my daughters and my church. And the faithful, precious church staff. They held me together and held the church together in the face of rumors, difficult transitions, and days filled with fear and worry as we tried to understand the will of God concerning us as a body of believers.

Days turned into weeks and weeks into months, and one day I realized that eight months had come and gone, and we had survived! The court of public opinion had declared that our church would only last six months. Observers both sympathetic and cynical waited for us to fail, even expected it. They had already written our epitaph, but God silenced their tongues and returned their empty utterances to them stamped "VOID."

Many people were ushered out of our lives. I thought satan had driven them out, but I realized, as time went on, that many had been "pruned" away by God Himself. A bigger tree is not always a better tree.

Sometimes there are branches that bear little fruit and spend more time sucking nutrients and sustenance from those that are fruitful. But when the Master Gardener gets His hands on such a tree, He wastes no time cutting away fruitless, excess limbs. That done, the tree is able to function more efficiently and grow healthier, and those branches that bore fruit become even more productive.

God guided us through the pruning process. He restored, reshaped, renewed, and revived New Bethel, and He made me pastor of a smaller, but faithful and fired-up congregation. Wayne Davis' shoes would be big ones to fill, I thought, but the Lord reassured me. If it had been His intent for Bishop Davis' shoes to be filled, Bishop Davis would be filling them. He had ushered in a new order. I didn't know what His plans were for our church, but I knew that I had been called to duty, and I would not disappoint the One who had been so faithful to see me through the most difficult valley of my life.

I prayed daily for His mercy. I drank liberally of His grace. I followed where He led me. The calamity of widowhood had birthed a new, deeper level of faith in me. I had thanked God so many times for seeing me through Wayne's death. Now I realized that his death was not just an end to his suffering and my happiness. It was the beginning of my preparation to take his shepherd's staff. How awesome is our God, who wastes nothing. Weeping becomes a well. Pain becomes compassion. Tragedy becomes testimony. Death is swallowed up in the victory of resurrection power!

In the early fall of 1993, I sent a delegation of church leaders to the Crystal Cathedral Annual Women's Conference in Garden Grove, California. Some weeks later, I was preparing to travel to Israel and called a 5 a.m. staff meeting at my home to make sure all was well before I left. During this meeting, Elder Dorcas Chandler was to report on the women's conference she and others had attended. Little did I realize that this staff meeting would be the beginning of new and exciting challenges in my life, both personally and in my ministry.

Celebrate Change

When Dorcas began sharing her report, the first thing I noticed was the folder she held in her hand. On the front of it, in clear bold lettering, was a title: "CELEBRATE CHANGE." As her recounting of the conference unfolded, God spoke quietly, but very clearly. The theme for our church in 1994 would be "Celebrate Change."

Celebrate change, did you say? My mind traveled quickly over the recent months. Change had been a most uncomfortable thing for me. My husband had died. My family's foundation had been torn from beneath them. Our church had lost a pastor, the community a leader. And now God was asking—no *telling*—me and my fragile congregation to celebrate change? Wouldn't it be easier to tell us to celebrate pain, tribulation, anxiety, catastrophe, and upheaval? But He only repeated the earlier edict. Celebrate change.

The staff meeting continued. I half listened and half considered what continued to echo inside me. Then, suddenly, the command became more intense, more vivid. Where the gentle mantra of "celebrate change" had echoed softly, the Word of God now thundered and demanded my full attention. *"Remember ye not the former things, neither consider the things of old. Behold, I will do a new thing; now it shall spring forth; shall ye not know it?..."* (Is. 43:18-19).

In that moment, I recognized that God was not merely mapping out the topic of conversation at a few luncheons or a church anniversary. This was a call to order. He had prepared us for a challenge and had already declared us victorious. Would we receive this blessing or miss it because we were unwilling to embrace the unknown? We had missed enough. We had already lost too much. We would not miss this.

I interrupted Elder Chandler's report to announce that God had given us our 1994 church theme, "Celebrate Change." I instructed them to have banners made with the theme and the Scripture the Lord had given us while I was away in Israel.

I saw on their faces what I felt in my heart. How do we celebrate change when the circumstances surrounding our change are so painful?

We had just buried our leader, and now, eight short months later, we are to celebrate? It seemed irreverent and shameless and even unkind.

I watched them as they took in my instructions. The doubt, which had been fading of late, was back on their faces. And even I faltered in the face of it. Part of me was screaming "No, no, no!" I could not celebrate my newly acquired station—from wife to widow, from married to single—as though it was a gift or a blessing. I was not glad to be a widow. This mantle of leadership was not one I chose. If I had chosen, my husband would be with me, healed and whole. And yet God continued to say, "Celebrate change."

The banners decorated the walls of our sanctuary. The staff was planning events around our new theme. But we had not embraced it. If it was a word from God, why was it not in the spirits of the congregation? The Lord showed me that sheep follow the shepherd. If my church was not ready to celebrate change, it was because I was not. I had done all the things the Lord had directed me to behaviorally, but my heart was not in it. My behavior alone was an incomplete act of obedience. In fact, because my behavior wasn't in line with my heart, my behavior was a lie. I was acting as though I had surrendered to God's command to celebrate change, but I was as resistant to it as I had always been.

One afternoon, I was driving to Harbor General Hospital to pray for one of our ministers. I was tired, discouraged, and feeling very weak under the weight of my responsibilities. Driving south on the 110 Freeway in Los Angeles, I distinctly remember looking up to Heaven and shouting, "God, I don't like this!" I didn't understand what He was doing. I didn't understand what He'd already done or why He did it! If He had to take one of us from earth to glory, why did He take Wayne? He was the visionary. He was the "pastor of pastors." He was the "shepherd of shepherds." Why did He leave me here on earth and take Wayne? Did He make a mistake? I continued to rail against the One who could wipe me and every other car off the freeway with a thought.

When He had had enough, He thundered back at me. "I have already instructed you to celebrate change. I am the Lord your God. I am sovereign. I do not have to explain My actions." I didn't respond, but in my heart, I still hurt. I could not imagine anything worse than what I was going through. But God imagined for me, and His response to me was swift. One thing worse would be for me to join my husband not having done what God had called me to do. "If I wanted Wayne left on earth, I could have left him on earth. I chose to close that chapter of life."

I immediately repented. I did not want the Lord to take me home too. And I did not want to leave here without finishing what I was put here to do. I wanted to hear Him say, "Well done, good and faithful servant." All God needed was my willing heart. That day He got it and together we began the journey to understanding how to recognize, discern, embrace, and eventually celebrate change.

The first gift on this path to celebrating change came quickly. The peace that I fought so hard to hold on to in the past, washed over me and rushed through me, settling my heart, clearing my mind, and calming my senses. I was still tired. I still didn't understand everything that was happening to me. I still felt the absence of my husband. But when I surrendered my will to God—when I determined that day to learn how to celebrate change and not just tolerate it—He made me a promise. He said He would not leave me or forsake me.

It was not the first time He had said that. It was not the first time I had believed Him for it. But it was the first time that I knew with certainty that *all* the changes in my life were good changes. It was the first time I was able to believe that I would be able to honor my husband and celebrate life without him at the same time. I didn't know how that would happen, but I knew that it would. I would learn how to receive and celebrate every change in my life, then teach others to do the same. First Apostolic would be a church that received, with gratitude and hallelujahs, every crook, turn, and wind in the road we were on.

This book is a collection of the gifts I received on the road to understanding how to celebrate change. Change is God's invitation to a blessing. Celebrating change prepares you to receive the blessing. I want to share my blessing with you. Change has not always been comfortable for me. It was not without its pain. I have struggled in it and labored to remember the promises of God through it. But because God is gracious,

I am stronger with each change. My faith grows from strength to strength. Mountains pack their bags when they see me coming. And each day finds me begging God to let His Kingdom come and let His will be done (in my life) on earth as it is in Heaven!

Changing Your Mind

Why do you suppose God wants us to celebrate change when there seems to be so much comfort in the familiar? Does He want us uncomfortable, fearful, uncertain, doubtful? No, He just wants us to trust Him. Think about it. Your faith is the cornerstone of your relationship with God. Think of your faith as a spiritual muscle and change as the machine that exercises your faith. It doesn't take much faith to do business as usual. The enemy would love to keep you content in yesterday's blessings in order to prevent you from seeking God's direction for your tomorrows. No change, no gain.

1. List three circumstances about your life that have changed in the past five years that you wish hadn't changed.

2. Take each circumstance and think about all the ways you have made it obvious, to God and others, that you do not accept the change.

3. Now, think about what you would do if you wanted to make it obvious, to God and others, that you *did* accept the change.

4. Imagine that you've traveled three miles and realize that you went one mile past your destination. By the time you back-track, how far have you traveled? You've gone *four* miles. You can't give back the extra mile you've traveled. And you wouldn't have arrived at your desired destination if you hadn't accepted the fact that you had missed your mark. The same is true of change. Accepting where you are is the first step to moving to where you want to be. Even getting "back to where you used to be" requires forward movement.

5. Think about the three circumstances again. Pray and ask God to show you how to move forward from them. Ask Him to give you a heart to do the things you listed in question #3.

6. Read Philippians 4:6-7, 12-13. Have you applied these Scriptures to your circumstances to help you cope with the changes they have brought?

"Once upon a time there was a woman named Wanda Ann who lived in California with her two daughters Wendy and Whitney..."

Change

Chapter Two

Beauty for Ashes

Thou hast turned for me my mourning into dancing: Thou hast put off my sackcloth, and girded me with gladness.

—Psalm 30:11

"The whole history of the Christian life is a series of resurrections... Every time a man finds his heart is troubled, that he is not rejoicing in God, a resurrection must follow; a resurrection out of the night of troubled thought into the gladness of the truth."

—George MacDonald

January 1994 ticked into existence at a special New Year's Eve celebration co-hosted by First Apostolic Church and its neighbor Faithful Central Baptist Church. I smiled to myself at how easily the denominational differences between the two churches became miniscule against the power of people united in worship.

Praise was high, and God graciously, mercifully, and wonderfully descended to meet us there in the auditorium of Washington Preparatory High School. He washed over and through us, bombarding our spiritual senses. Some knew Him in those moments as Jehovah-Jireh, the Lord whose miraculous provision made an indelible mark on 1993. Others had found peace in that year and chose the last moments of it, amidst the din of exaltation and thanksgiving, to share quiet communion with the Savior in the privacy of their own hearts.

Then there were those who wore their broken spirits for all to see, praising God "in spite of," "in the midst of," and "because of" the devastation and desolation in their lives. Their faces were like jagged stones for much of the service, stubbornly refusing to remember the God who had obviously forgotten them. But my Lord who knows all things desired to meet them there that night to whisper in their ears, "Precious lamb, I know the plans I have for you...." He led them to the valley of their own unshed tears where He had built a well. "Draw out," was all He told them. And as they cried out to Him, daring to believe one more time that He could and would save them, they were refreshed.

I am always so awed by the miracle of a resurrected spirit. To earthly eyes, tears are little more than punctuation for the statement of sorrow. But spiritual eyes discern the process of restoration, the rushing of angels and of God Himself to the aid of the one lost, hurt, afraid, or dying. It is one of those odd and incredible paradoxes of the Kingdom that the smoldering wick of the spirit is not extinguished, but ignited when we release the flood of our tears.

Satisfied that the Lord was moving powerfully on behalf of all the saints who had come to cross the threshold of the New Year with Him, I allowed myself to indulge in a little personal reflection. I considered all the new assignments I had been given that year. I was now a widow, a single mother, a single woman, a pastor, and a Christian community leader. I thought about our church theme for the coming year: "Celebrate Change." My mind attempted to wrap itself around the new relationships and responsibilities that would reshape my life.

I remember sitting on the stage, as the service seemed to move along around me, prioritizing my future. I once heard Loraine Daniels, a minister from Texas, preach on prioritizing. She said we must get to a place in life where we can ask and answer the following questions: What is

18

important to me? Who is important to me? She said all meaningful living demands that we come to terms with those two things. So I found myself grappling with those two queries. *What is important to me? Who is important to me?* My answers to those questions had changed so drastically since Wayne's death.

Often we are challenged to prioritize our lives during difficult times or circumstances that seem insurmountable. We are required to interrupt cycles of grief, pain, and anger to get our lives together. Alongside the troubles that confront us, the Word of God confronts us more aggressively and reminds us that God is faithful to do whatever He has promised. Isaiah 49:14-16 illustrates a wonderful promise from God to each of us. Israel said, "The Lord has forsaken us and forgotten us." But the Lord told Isaiah to say to Israel, "Can a woman forget her nursing child? She may, but I will not forget you. Behold, I have inscribed you upon the palms of My hands."

When I was in grade school, we'd have tests. Some kids took the time to study, but others prepared for the test by writing some of the answers on their hands to help them remember. God's got His own little system worked out for the tests of our lives. He just has to look at His hand, and He remembers you. Not just your name, but *you*. Everything you are, want, need, face, or fear is right there for Him to see. That gives us a new perspective on the song "He's Got the Whole World in His Hand."

It matters not how desperate we are for relief. Help is always on the way and on time because God does not forget us. That's why we can "count it all joy" when we fall into divers temptations, troubles, and circumstances (see Jas. 1:2). In other words, we can start the party in the midst of our peril because we know victory is on the way. Think differently, reconsider your behavior, and reprogram yourself to keep a good attitude, having faith in God and His Word.

My heart lifted as I ruminated on how faithful God had been to me over the past year, and I looked forward to the grace He would afford me to face the coming year. Suddenly, I was struck with a startling realization. The desire for order had reentered me.

One of the hallmarks of my grief had been the frustrating tendency of my mind to refuse to settle on the painful actuality that my life would never be the same again. I could think about everything that was happening in my life, even function in my new duties efficiently and seemingly without great effort. But I was living day to day. I woke up every morning and decided that, Lord willing, I would make it through the next 24 hours. And when I retired to bed, I could say no more than, "Today was a good day," or "Today was not a good day." If I thought too far into the future, fear threatened to overtake me. Even my decision to celebrate change was lived in faith. Because God had said I would do it, I believed I would, even if I couldn't think ahead to how I would. Psalm 92:1-2 says it's a good thing to thank the Lord and praise Him for His loving-kindness every morning, and His faithfulness every night. Sometimes that's all we can do.

But here I was, without resisting, putting what I knew about my future in order. I look back on that evening and think about how we have to catch up to our faith in order for change to occur. God has to tell us where we're going, then get us there through a series of seen and unseen processes.

When you get in your car to go somewhere, you use the key to start it up, and it moves when you take it out of park and put your foot on the gas. But how much thought do you give to the engine, the transmission, the pistons, the fuel, the fuel injectors, spark plugs, brake fluid, fan belt, radiator, battery, and a thousand other things that work in concert to get you and your car from here to there? All the time I spent trying to force myself to embrace change was fruitless because only God knew how broken my heart was and what it would take to get it back in "working order."

Celebrating change is an act of our will. But it cannot occur until we accept change, and that requires the work of God through His Holy Spirit. When I gave everything up to God, that did not suddenly make me able to celebrate change. My surrender was a signal to God and the world that I was *ready*. Then God set out to make me able. He put me on the path to becoming one who would be capable of celebrating change. And the first stop on that path was making peace with the truth that change had arrived.

What had God commissioned me to do? Well, in addition to His direct command to celebrate change, the Lord constantly assigned me to Isaiah 61:1-3 as a reference for my "job description."

> *The Spirit of the Lord God is upon Me, because the Lord has anointed Me to preach good tidings to the poor; He has sent Me to heal the brokenhearted, to proclaim liberty to the captives, and the opening of the prison to those who are bound; to proclaim the acceptable year of the Lord, and the day of vengeance of our God; to comfort all who mourn, to console those who mourn in Zion, to give them beauty for ashes, the oil of joy for mourning, the garment of praise for the spirit of heaviness...* (Isaiah 61:1-3 NKJV).

Over and over again the words "to give them beauty for ashes" echoed in my heart. As I looked out over the people gathered in His name, I prayed silently, *Lord, are You really going to give us beauty for ashes? There is so much in my life that doesn't appear beautiful right now. There is so much reparation still to be done in the wake of First Apostolic's upheaval and so much peace to cultivate within and among its frightened and struggling flock.* And still, in the midst of my uncertain petitions, He repeated, "to give them beauty for ashes." So I allowed Him to speak more to my spirit concerning this word.

Isaiah 61 begins with a list of things we can expect from God when His Spirit rests upon us. The poor (in spirit) receive the good news (the gospel). The brokenhearted are tended to. Captives are freed and those bound are loosed. Soon though, the declarations become commerce. Exchanges begin to take place: beauty for ashes, gladness for mourning, and praise for heaviness. We are required to participate actively in the exchange called for by God. We give Him something, and He gives us something in return. So God would give me beauty when I gave Him my ashes. Well…where would these ashes come from?

There was something significant about ashes that I needed to look at. I found it in Isaiah 48:10 where God says, "Behold, I have refined thee, but not with silver; I have chosen thee in the furnace of affliction." In other words, He allowed the fires of affliction to come upon you. He gave satan permission to touch your life with trouble. And when satan used the flames of trouble to incinerate and devastate you and everything familiar to you, he left you a heap of ashes. The world looked at you and waited for the wind to blow you away or someone to come and sweep you away with the rubbish. But before any of that could happen, God stopped by, stooped down into the furnace, and found you. He saw you and said, "Now I've got something to work with." In that moment He chose to put your life on display for His glory.

What are ashes? They are the unburned particles and grayish powder left after a thing has been burned. They are the ruins or remains of something destroyed. The furnace of affliction is full of ruined and destroyed lives. To the world, it looks like nothing. In reality, it is the workshop from which God crafts His most miraculous and glorious works of art. Second Corinthians 4:17 sums it up like this: "For our light affliction, which is but for a moment, worketh for us a far more exceeding and eternal weight of glory."

As I looked back over my life since Wayne's death, I wondered many times how the Lord would get the glory out of my "light affliction" (which really felt more heavy than light). I knew God was very aware of my circumstances. Though I found it hard to "lean not to my own understanding" at times, I did acknowledge Him in all my ways and believed He was directing my path.

In fact, before I married Wayne Sylvester Davis, I sought God in prayer and fasting, and He confirmed and affirmed that yes, I was to marry this man. And yet God, being omniscient—knowing all at all times—knew way back on April 5, 1969, that 24 years later on April 16,

1993, that my husband would die of a most debilitating disease, leaving behind questions, pain, hurt, shame, and anger. And yet, God said yes, marry him. Job said "[God] knoweth the way that I take: when He hath tried me, I shall come forth as gold" (Job 23:10).

If you look at God's handiwork throughout Scripture—in the temple and in the New Jerusalem, for example—you'll find that whenever He works with gold, it's always pure gold. In other words, He only uses gold that is free from impurities or other metals. In order for gold to be purified, it has to be heated until it melts and all the impurities, which are not as heavy as the gold itself, rise to the top and are drawn off.

Our affliction, which is "lighter" than the "weight" of the glory of eternal life with God, is brought to the surface when the fire of adversity is allowed to rage in our lives. Well, Lord knows I had been in the fire. I had been in the flames and my affliction was there for the world to see. My life was a pile of ashes. And my hope rested in a promise from God that He would exchange the ashes for beauty; that my desolation would become deliverance and my grief would become a glorious testimony.

The crises, the troubles, the losses, the embarrassments, and the struggles that satan brings to our lives usher us into the furnace of affliction. And those troubles and trials that satan has meant to destroy us, instead burn us down to a place where "the things that can be shaken will be shaken so that those that cannot be shaken can remain" (see Heb. 12:27). They burn us down into what appears to be ruined and destroyed lives. But that's where God declares, "I'm going to give you beauty for everything broken, stolen, marred, or desecrated by satan in your life. Everything burned up—dreams, visions, marriages, finances, ministries, health—I'm going to return to you in glorious condition."

I have a friend who leased a car in 1997. Because she didn't understand the fundamentals of leasing, she used a broker who promised to get her a good deal. She put $5,000.00 down on the car, and her monthly payments were still very high. Her circumstances drastically changed soon after she got the car. She only earned about a seventh of what she used to earn. In the next three years she had a major surgery, found herself on unemployment, and suffered a broken engagement.

Then God told her to clean out her car and return it to the dealer. It had a scratch on the side and some on the bumper (so much for the security deposit she had put on the car). She went to turn in her car, not knowing what she would do for transportation. All God would say to her on the way was, "Trust Me."

She returned from the dealer with a brand-new 2001 model of the same car. She had put only $300 down on this one, and her monthly payments were $55 *less* per month than they were on the other car. She had had credit problems in the past and was forced to pay a high interest rate to a finance company at a time when she was earning six figures. This time, she was instantly approved by the dealer at a special low interest rate.

"I was so arrogant when I leased the car the first time. They told me what to pay, and I threw my money at them to prove that a black woman could pay whatever it took to get whatever she wanted. Then God allowed everything I had to be taken away from me. By the time I had to bring that car back, all I said was, 'Lord, if You want me on the bus, I'll do it.' By the time I got to the dealer, I already knew what I could pay for a car, but it was so much less than I had paid for the car I already had. And God went under that amount! The new car is even nicer than the one I had before. But this time, I wasn't throwing my money around. This time, I knew it was God's money, and I gave it gratefully, almost in tears." Beauty for ashes.

The furnace houses within its fiery den a hidden promise. It is a promise of restoration, a promise to bless you where it seems you were cursed, empowerment where you appear to be weakened. All of us want God's good, great and wonderful, glorious blessings bestowed upon us. And we should want God's blessings. But few of us want to pay the price for blessedness. Some blessings only come by way of affliction. And while we endure, we must endure convinced that all our grief, sorrow, and confusion will soon yield a bountiful harvest. Through prayer and faith, we must believe a change is on the way and soon we will be able to celebrate as God turns what was meant for evil into good.

During that most difficult year of my life, I was blessed by a message prophetically preached by my brother-in-law Rev. Troy Dockery. He stood so anointed and sure as he ministered from the text and subject, "The Latter Shall Be Greater Than the Former." As he spoke, it was God's voice I heard. I was one of many listening, but I knew God was speaking specifically to me, the widow of Wayne Davis, pastor of First Apostolic Church, single mother struggling.

When people were leaving and transferring membership from the church, God said, "the latter shall be greater than the former." When I experienced the rejection of my late husband's family, my in-laws, God said, "the latter shall be greater than the former." When finances seemed crazy and budgets reflected more need than net, He reminded me again, "the latter shall be greater than the former." When sons and daughters in the ministry began opening their own churches with members from our "home" church, God comforted me repeatedly with, "the latter shall be greater than the former."

And when I sat huddled on the floor in front of my bedroom fireplace, lonely, scared, feeling like a hollow "single shell" of a formerly married woman…a whisper gently brushed along my fragile, faltering heart, only loud enough to become the faintest hope. *The latter shall be greater than the former, precious one.*

That faint glimmer of hope was enough to ignite my spirit that New Year's Eve. I had been straining to hear something—anything—that would make sense of my situation. So when God spoke of exchanging beauty for ashes, I was a ready hearer. Even before I knew what He wanted to do with the ashes of my life, I was gathering them up to give to Him. I was not one who wanted to sit amongst ashes any longer than I had to. There are some who prefer the familiarity of the ashes to whatever beauty God promises. That's why some women will stay in an abusive relationship. Fear is very powerful. And satan will have you so afraid to face the unknown that you'll be willing to choke on the desolation around you.

Two weeks into widowhood, I attended the bridal shower of a dear, beloved friend of mine, Carolyn Harrell. During that special gathering, no less than six beautiful women of God prophesied, "This that we do for Carolyn, soon we shall do for you. You shall be married again very soon." It was as though God was saying, "Wipe your eyes and put on your dancing slippers, child, because weeping may endure for a night, but joy cometh in the morning!" A part of me became immediately excited. I even had a gentleman all picked out who I just knew was the will of God concerning my life (of course I was wrong about him). But was it possible that God was about to give me a new miracle of love, joy, and hope?

I recall one afternoon standing in a terminal at San Jose Airport on my way to a conference. I glanced to my right and saw a young couple hugging and holding one another. I allowed myself a moment to miss similar moments in my past. Then I distinctly heard satan declare, "Forget it. You will never experience that again." It was like a slap in the face. I was surprised to find tears in my eyes.

As I wiped the tears away, I tried to recall the words of prophecy that had been spoken over my life. "You shall marry again soon." "The latter shall be greater than the former." *But how, Lord? You told me I was not to date or be seen running all over the city and country with a lot of different men. How will I be blessed to experience the fellowship of a love relationship if I can't even date?*

To be honest, there were times when I wasn't even sure I wanted to be married again, especially if there was a chance that the same kind of pain I had experienced could repeat itself. There were many days and nights that I wanted to tell God, "I give up. Stop the music. Take Your lovely serenades of hope and give me back my tissues." I wanted so desperately to ask God if I could have some guarantees to go with His promises, a little more concrete idea of His plans for me. But during that difficult time, my sense of God was so real, so clear. In my heart, I knew

He had spoken. And I knew if He had spoken, then He would perform, and all would be revealed to me in due season.

Often, as if sensing my trepidation, the Lord would whisper, "Behold, I shall do a new thing." I would look up at the Lord and say, "Lord, can't You see I'm still trying to recover from the old thing?" Initially, I kicked and screamed, cried and complained as God began changing the very complexion of my life as a woman, mother, and minister. My church had begun changing. My adult children began changing. Even my physical appearance changed. I worried God with endless questions about where He was taking me and what He was doing with me. Finally, I realized that God really wasn't trying to destroy or hurt me. He was trying to bless me beyond measure. All I had to do was be willing to change, again and again.

I began to submit myself to the hands of the Master Potter. I began to activate my faith. God had declared through His vessels that I would marry again. I took Him at His word. I went home and, with the assistance of two precious friends in Christ, began redecorating my master bedroom suite. I changed the carpet. I changed the theme colors of the rooms. I changed the bedding and some of the furnishings. Then I took myself on a special shopping trip to see my friends at Victoria's Secret. I filled six drawers with new lingerie and intimate wear, preparing for this new man and new marriage God had promised. And once my room and wardrobe were complete, I shut the door to that room and determined not to use it until I married again.

During this season in my life, I really thought I had let go of past hurts, past memories, and past devastation. In actuality, I was not only still holding onto it, but it had become a part of me. I was walking around like a porter at a train station or a skycap at the airport. Hauling around baggage occupied much of my waking hours.

Of course, I had packed all my bags very neatly. If you knew I had baggage at all, you were sure it was just a carry-on, nothing major. I walked through most days the picture of emotional, spiritual, physical, psychological, and social health. Nobody's smile was brighter than mine.

I was busy and productive. I had even convinced myself that I was "through the valley." The baggage was, after all, out of sight, so I had put it out of my mind.

What began happening though, with increasing regularity, was that I was often thrown into mental and emotional tailspins, explosions, and mood swings whenever I bumped into moments or memories from my past. An insensitive comment, a sound, a situation, gossip that rerouted itself to my ears—so much debris from the most painful episode of my life—became triggers that set me off. And my reactions were intensified by the pressure I was exerting on myself to "keep it all together."

Keep it together for my kids who are still so afraid. Keep it together for the church that had lost its bearings. Keep it together for my friends who are so worried about me. Keep it together just to rub it in the faces of all those people who are waiting for me to fail. Keep it together for the memory of Wayne Sylvester Davis. Keep it together for everybody but Wanda, who needed so desperately to let it go, pour it out, collapse, cry, scream, and just get a good night's sleep!

It was during this time of my life that I had to face the fact that I had not let go of anything. In fact, I was holding onto things with a death grip. It's interesting, that phrase "death grip"—particularly as it applied to me. Like I said, being ready to celebrate change doesn't make you able. Once I told God I was ready to embrace change, He had to show me the areas in me that were resistant to it. He showed me that there was "stuff" associated with my marriage and life *before* Wayne's death that I had not released.

In fact, the baggage I was carrying was piled on top of other baggage that had become a foundation for the new baggage. And I knew when I saw it that unless I unpacked all those bags, my husband's death would have a grip on me, even as I held on. But Jesus had a word for someone just like me. He said, "Come unto Me, all ye that labour and are heavy laden, and I will give you rest" (Mt. 11:28). Oh, how I needed rest. So I went to Him.

I thought about how God had told me He would "do a new thing." I looked up the Scripture. It's worth seeing that one, Isaiah 43:19, and the one which comes immediately before it:

Remember ye not the former things, neither consider the things of old. Behold, I will do a new thing; now it shall spring forth; shall ye not know it? I will even make a way in the wilderness, and rivers in the desert (Isaiah 43:18-19).

I really like the New Living Translation:

Forget all that—it's nothing compared to what I am going to do. For I am about to do a brand-new thing. See, I have already begun! Do you not see it? I will make a pathway through the wilderness for My people to come home. I will create rivers for them in the desert!

You know I was shouting and tried to dance until my feet fell off! Everything I needed was right there. I needed something new. I needed a pathway through the wilderness of heartbreak to healing. I needed a drink to refresh and restore me in my emotional desert. And I needed to know that the process had already begun.

But in order to get on with life, we must get to a new place in our hearts where we are willing to "remember not the former things." For unless you are willing to release the old, you can never come into the new. In fact, the greatest enemy of the new is the old. The greatest enemy of our destiny is our history.

Paul helped me out with this in his letter to the church at Philippi. He said, "Brethren, I count not myself to have apprehended: but this one thing I do, forgetting those things which are behind, and reaching forth unto those things which are before" (Phil. 3:13). Satan recognizes the importance of destiny (even if we don't). And often he attacks us today for where we're headed tomorrow.

Now I don't believe satan is omniscient. I don't believe he knows what God has planned for me. But he does have enough sense to know God does have a plan. God had a plan when he made satan. But that serpent is just prideful enough to think he can thwart the plan of God. (It's interesting that there is a Greek word rendered "pride" in the Bible that also means "blind" and "stupid." Hmm.)

As I began living out the text just quoted, I discovered that I, Wanda, had not yet "attained." I had not yet arrived. I hadn't grasped, understood, or discerned fully all that I would need to know as a new pastor, single parent, or single woman. But I was clear on one thing. I could get to a place where I would think no more of, remember not, lose sight of, discount, dismiss, disregard, ignore, omit, overlook, and consign to oblivion all those "things" (historical events, issues, circumstances, situations, troubles, and private pains) that were behind me. And they were behind me, no matter what the father of lies was whispering in my ear.

I was ready to reach forth for the things that were before me. I was ready to go get all the blessings God laid out in His Word yesterday for my tomorrow, which included His plan to prosper, help, heal, and keep me. I began to remember that I had the destiny that was spoken of in Jeremiah 29:11. He knows the thoughts that He thinks toward me. They are thoughts of peace and not evil, to give me a future and a hope.

When you make up your mind to forget those things that are behind, God doesn't waste any time filling up those empty spaces with His Word. I had new "baggage." Big, pretty Louis Vuitton steamer trunks, full of the Holy Ghost and light as a feather. In them were peace, joy, comfort, power, strength, hope, confidence, faith, and love. And I could go into them and pull out whatever I needed. God's decision to change my church was not to devastate me, but to establish a new vision for a new people facing a new day. I no longer had to apologize for modifying or changing anything Bishop Wayne Davis had established in his vision. I only had to be strong enough and willing enough to become an Esther "for such a time as this."

I began to realize that God's promise of a new love, a new life, and a new marriage was not to dishonor or negate the 24 years of love and marriage I had with Wayne. But He wanted to give me a new love, a new marriage, and a new relationship for the new season He had placed me in. Once I was able to grasp and understand this, I was set free to walk into my destiny. The Spirit of the Lord was upon me. But I learned in this season that in order to set captives free and release those in bondage, you must first be willing to be free yourself. In order to preach good tidings to the poor, you must first be a testimony of what you're testifying, otherwise you're just peddling words without truth.

Then something else became crystal clear for me. I could not begin building new memories or experiencing new joys until I took active steps to leave the old behind. That would be achieved through a process that involves the heart and the mind. With my mind I needed to forget. With my heart I needed to forgive. Both involve circumstance and choice. I had to come to a place in life where my heart had come into agreement with my mind about all that had gone on in my life. Only then would I be able to move on.

This agreement was easier to process than to practice. My mind was more than ready to move on with my life. The problem was my heart didn't want to follow. My heart hung on stubbornly to past memories of people, places, and things, both good and bad. In the chambers of my heart were events and circumstances that I didn't want to let go of. There were injustices that I wanted righted before I would close the chapter on them. There were circumstances that couldn't be reversed, and I held onto my desire for them like a petulant child. I silently nagged God, asking Him, "Why can't things be different than they are?" He had long answered me, but I kept asking every time I refused to let go of my past.

For a while, God let me hold on. He was willing to allow me to stay stuck in yesterday's goals, achievements, misfortunes, tears, and relationships. And I learned the hard way that no one cares to hear about your yesterdays for very long, not even God. Eventually, He becomes silent. He won't join you in your private pity parties anymore. He will not overstep your will to remain stuck. He will watch you chain yourself to painful, devastating memories and past accomplishments until you are tired of hearing yourself talk about them. He'll wait until you are sincerely ready to turn them loose and receive the new and exciting changes waiting just for you.

My decision to move on began with a visit to the cemetery. There I opened my heart to God's Word concerning forgiveness. Forgiving begins with a decision to let go of or put behind us people, places, and things too painful to live with. When we forgive, we make a decision in our hearts to set people free who hurt us, angered us, or harmed us. We are motivated in part by the understanding that our heavenly Father forgives us as we forgive others. That means He forgives us *in the same manner* that we forgive others. If I am zealous about holding on to wrongs done to me, how much more zealous would God be when it came to excusing me?

I stood weeping at the grave of my deceased spouse, forgiving him and many others for past hurt and pain. I forgave them for everything I had charged to their account. "I forgive you for dying, Wayne!" I cried aloud. How could that be his fault? And yet, I had blamed him for the pain his dying had caused me. I was so angry with him for leaving me here, so angry that he had left our children. The more I forgave, the more it seemed I had to forgive. A dam had burst somewhere in me and the flood of blame, injured pride, ire, sadness, regret, shame, loneliness, and frustration that I had been harboring against my husband and people whom I felt betrayed me came rushing forth. And I did not stop until I had released it all. What a liberating experience it was!

Perhaps the most amazing thing about it was the clarity that immediately followed. There were people I could not trust or feel comfortable around because I had not forgiven them. There were situations and circumstances that would automatically depress or anger me because I had not forgiven the people or things I associated with them. When the deluge subsided and peace had returned to me, I saw clearly whom I could trust with my heart. Before, I couldn't trust anybody. I was an open wound, and I wouldn't let anybody get anywhere close to my raw, vulnerable heart. My perspective of those who had hurt me was even different. They were hurting me out of their own emotional pain. Most of them were not innately cruel, just broken inside and malfunctioning. (Of course, some of them were downright mean, but I forgave them and left

32

them for God to handle.) I left the cemetery feeling 20 years younger and 30 pounds lighter.

We can only move forward when we embrace the truth of the Scripture that exhorts us to "let this mind be in you, which was also in Christ Jesus" (Phil. 2:5). Now, the mind of Christ Jesus is illogical and consistently inconsistent and irrational to our earthly rationalizing. It just doesn't make sense sometimes. The mind of Christ surpasses all understanding and operates in the reverse of all we think, for God is a being of grace and mercy, and often we are not. God hates sin but loves the sinner. We hate sinners but love sin. God accepts; we reject. God is compassionate and is known to be "the Healer." Man is often brutal and called "a killer." We want God to come on our time, and He comes *in His time*. We look past people's needs to see their faults. Jesus looked past our faults and saw our need.

The mind of Christ, I found, is beyond my reason. It's absurd, confounding, and puzzling. In fact, the mind of Christ boggles my mind. You will get a headache trying to figure Him out. In times of drought, Jesus says go fishing and let down your nets. We destroy marriages with fornication. Jesus destroys fornication with marriage. Jesus says if you want life, be willing to die. If you want to rule, be a servant. If you want to be mature in your faith, act like a child. Rejoice in tribulation. Love those who hate you.

If you're crippled, you should know that you can walk. If you believe you're the one doing the walking, you're going to fall. If you want to receive, give. On earth, seeing is believing. In the spirit realm, believing is seeing, because faith is the substance of things hoped for, the evidence of things not seen (see Heb. 11:1). What a God we serve. And in order to receive a godly blessing, we must think and see the way He does, then do accordingly.

I realized that when I gave myself permission to operate in the mind-set of Christ, I could forgive people and forget situations that would hinder me from running this race. If God could forgive the world, and His power lives in me, then I can forgive. How? The same way He does—*He chooses to*! I made a decision that I would not let unforgiveness prevent me from reaching my destiny.

You cannot remember and forget at the same time, just as you cannot forgive and indict at the same time. You can't drive a new car and an old jalopy at the same time. You must get rid of the old to drive the new. God cannot and will not bless you in a new relationship with fidelity, trust, and romance, until you get rid of that past life that hovers over your every action and reaction.

When we celebrate, we joyfully and openly acknowledge the presence or the existence of something or someone with thanks or appreciation. God wants us to celebrate change, not just tolerate it. A celebration is something to look forward to. And you can't look forward and backward at the same time. Once I understood that, I was ready and anxious to receive a beautiful future in exchange for the ashes of my past. But there was still more work to be done, and the Lord set about preparing me for it.

Change Your Mind

It seems like such an easy thing to "forget those things that are behind" and "press forward unto those things that are before." But the two don't happen simultaneously. I can't move forward until I have let go. That means there's a frightening space of darkness between letting go and going forth. That's the part that requires our faith. God's not going to contaminate your new blessing with the decay of things He has long declared dead in your life.

Close your eyes and imagine a baby's first steps. He uses a table or something else to get up and stabilize himself. Daddy waits across the room, close enough to get to, but too far to reach without letting go of the safety of the furniture. Your Daddy in Heaven is waiting for you.

1. What are the ashes in your life? What are those dreams, visions, and relationships that have been destroyed? What trials have shaken you emotionally, physically, or mentally? What or who has died and left you alone? List these things.

2. As clearly as you can, write how your life has changed for the worse and what you would do to "fix" your present circumstances regarding each thing.

3. Now, take the list and pray about it. Tell God exactly what you want and why. Moreover, express your pain, guilt, anger, frustration, confusion, and uncertainty to Him.

4. We struggle with change in our lives for one of three reasons. 1) We think God doesn't know our situation. 2) We think God doesn't care about our situation. 3) We think that even if He knew and cared, He could not do anything about our situation. Write each of these reasons at the top of a sheet of paper, then sort out your issues, placing them on the page that best describes why you're struggling.

5. Read Psalm 139:1-13, then write it out on the page that carries the heading, "God doesn't know about my situation."

6. Read Romans 8:31, 35-39, then write it out on the page where you have written, "God doesn't care about my situation."

7. Read Jeremiah 32:17, Luke 1:37, Ephesians 1:18-21, and Philippians 4:13, then write them out on the page titled, "God can't do anything about my situation."

8. Look at your three lists. Be as truthful as you can. Do you believe what you have written at the top of each page, or do you believe God's Word? Don't answer too quickly. Belief is fleshed out in behavior. Faith (belief) without works (behavior) is dead (see Jas. 2). Before we can deal with change, we have to understand our attitude about it. If you don't really believe these Scriptures—and it is all right if you don't; I don't know anyone with perfect faith—then confess and repent of your unbelief. You've made a great start.

"Once upon a time there was a woman named Wanda Ann who lived in California with her two daughters Wendy and Whitney and their husbands Steven and Timothy…"

Change

Chapter Three

A Minister, a Mouse, and a Miracle

The wilderness and the solitary place shall be glad for them;
and the desert shall rejoice, and blossom as the rose.

—Isaiah 35:1

"Your adversary would love for you to assume the worst about your situation. He would enjoy seeing you heave a sigh and resign yourself to feelings of depression. However, it's been my experience that when God is involved, anything can happen. The One who directed that stone in between Goliath's eyes and split the Red Sea down the middle and leveled the wall around Jericho and brought His Son back from beyond takes delight in mixing up the odds as He alters the inevitable and bypasses the impossible."

—Charles Swindoll

Bishop Benjamin Reid seemed to be larger than life to me sometimes. Everything about him was ample and abundant, as if God had just given him extra helpings of everything. Physically he was a big man, imposing and powerful. Even when his failing health would not permit him to stand or walk for more than a short while, he never took on the frailty of many who suffer debilitation.

In the years after he retired from his pastorate at First Church of God, he would elect to preach from time to time at particular churches and events where he had a special love for a pastor or a cause. He was carried to the pulpit and preached from a wheelchair, but he never allowed sympathy to be wasted on his condition. Often he began to speak before the applause quieted. His booming voice would break through every sound, every thought, every distraction. "I will," he thundered, "Bless the Lord AT ALL TIMES! And His praise shall CON-TIN-U-AL-LY BE IN MY MOUTH!"

It was his truth, his triumph, his testimony, his blessing to us all, and his instruction. It was a battle cry for everyone who believed. And as those words rose up in us, Dr. Reid, caught up in the majesty and glory of the Lord who seemed to inhabit him fully, would proclaim, "*Oh magnify the Lord with me! Let us exalt His name together*!" And we did, because we couldn't help it.

He was the embodiment of abundant life. His smile was the radiant gift of his generous heart. His counsel was poured forth from the wells of God's wisdom and not his own, so it was ever flowing and overflowing. You could not know him and not know his love for his family, particularly his wife Pearl, whom he usually introduced as "The Pearl of Great Price." His "sons and daughters" in the ministry included some of the most prominent and powerful preachers and teachers in the country. When he retired, one of them asked for "a double portion" of his spirit. When he died, that same pastor wept openly before thousands and declared that he felt like he was "outside in the rain without an umbrella" because the man who had so faithfully fathered him in ministry was now gone.

Bishop Ben Reid was a wonderful, kind, humble jewel of a man. Most people live their entire lives only hearing about men like him. I was blessed to call him father and friend. God placed him in my life to encourage and sustain me—and to remind me that God was truly God, no matter what my circumstances looked like.

One afternoon, shortly after my husband's death, we sat together sipping tea and chatting about some of everything and a lot of nothing. Then, quite suddenly, I found myself again on the precipice of a dark and recurring fear. I voiced it, for the first time, to Dr. Reid. I could not believe that anyone would want to spend the rest of his life with me. I was so afraid that I would forever be "the widow of Bishop Wayne Sylvester Davis," no one's wife, no one's sweetheart, no one's "pearl of great price."

Saying it out loud showed me my own fragility and, for a moment, I wasn't sure how I was being held together inside. Bishop Reid's rich laughter was salve poured on my open wound. "Don't worry about that. If anything, we'll have to run the brothers off!"

Just like that, I was free. Satan had me believing that when I buried my husband, I had buried my future and any dreams I had of being "Mrs. Anybody" ever again. But God sent a man with eyes to see beyond my fear and through him gave me another measure of faith. There are so many wonderful people placed in the Body of Christ to encourage, inform, challenge, confront, and comfort us when we are in the process of change. It's easy to forget sometimes that the earth is the Lord's and everything in it. He places desires in our hearts, then proceeds to move the universe to grant them. But God knows how forgetful we are. So He sends a friend, a brother or sister, a book, a rainbow, a memory, or a song to remind us that He holds our time, all our time, in His hands.

Change begins with a desire. That desire becomes a choice. That choice is then placed, by faith, in the hands of Almighty God. Once in His hands, it ceases to be controlled by people or circumstances. What we see begins to lie to us about what we heard God say. How often have you prayed to God for something, looked at your circumstances, your past, or your present situation and decided that your prayer didn't have a future? Sometimes the only thing separating us from what we want is our faith. I was looking at my situation and wondering if that was God's answer to me. But God doesn't show you something and then speak on it. He speaks, waits for you to believe, then shows you that you did in fact hear Him.

Psalm 77 speaks of the comfort that comes from God when we're feeling forsaken and forgotten. The writer cries his plight out to God and begs for a response. Then he is reminded of His mighty works and decides to meditate on them. Verse 18 says, "The voice of Thy thunder was in the heaven: the lightnings lightened the world: the earth trembled and shook."

Have you ever looked up at the sky during a thunderstorm? You see the sky light up and then count the seconds until you hear the thunder. Thunder and lightning don't seem to occur together because light travels faster than sound, so it reaches us first and sound follows. Seeing, then hearing. That's how it is here on earth, but not with God. Psalm 77:18 says we *hear* God's voice, then we *see* lightning. Throughout Scripture, God speaks, then allows His words to come to pass. And since we know that He's the same yesterday, today, and forever, we know that He's still operating like that today (see Heb. 13:8). He speaks, we hear, we believe, we see. Faith is the substance of things *not seen*, but faith comes by *hearing* (see Heb. 11:1; Rom. 10:17). What are you hearing God say that is getting lost under what you see?

Shortly after my time with Bishop Reid, on the eve of Thanksgiving, 1993, I got a call from a minister who lived in the East, Andrew C. Turner II. I didn't know him personally, but I did recognize his name because he had served as the international youth chairman of the Pentecostal Assemblies of the World, a Christian organization that our church was once affiliated with. He also had called following Wayne's death to offer my daughters and me his prayers and condolences.

I had once spoken at a conference Andrew had presided over in New Mexico, and I knew that he served as ruling elder and assistant pastor to a very dear friend and pastor, Bishop T.W. Weeks in Wilmington, Delaware. He served in that capacity for more than 13 years, and I often served as a guest speaker at their women's retreats. But in all that time, I

44

probably spoke to Andrew Turner only once or twice. I never met his former wife or either of his two children in all that time. But that November day he called, and in minutes we were laughing and talking like old buddies.

He told me that he was starting a new ministry in New Jersey on April 3, 1994. I was stunned for a moment, because April 3rd is my birthday. He went on to say that God had told him not to open the doors to his new church until he spoke with Dr. Wanda Davis in California.

I found that more than a little amusing. Why would God have him speak to me? I was the newest pastor on the block. I was making a million mistakes, and things were far from settled at First Apostolic. I was just getting used to my "shepherd's shoes," and my toes were getting stepped on a lot by angry sheep. "I love the people of God," I had told him, "but right now, I don't like many of them." Still, he insisted, he wanted to make an appointment to speak to me before opening his new church. He wanted to know when it would be convenient for him to fly out and meet with me.

I was doing a lot of traveling during the holidays. I told him my children and I would be spending Thanksgiving in Hawaii, so we were leaving the next day. Afterwards, I was scheduled to leave for Israel. When I returned, I had meetings scheduled and plans to make to finalize our annual Watch Night Celebration, which we would be co-hosting with another church. It was a big, complicated gathering. I told him I probably couldn't see him until January. He was so polite, kind, and gentle in his response. "That's fine. What day in January?" was all he said.

After checking with my office, we set January 5, 1994, for our meeting, and the conversation became fun and friendly again with a naturalness that surprised me. We laughed and talked about so many things. He shared with me that being a pastor was not something he really wanted to do, but he knew God was calling him to it.

His desire to do an excellent job for the Lord was obvious, and I told him, "If you want something you have never had, you must be willing to do something you have never done. So, you say you desire a church that is different, fresh, anointed, and exciting…then decide to seek the Lord Jesus for direction and instructions. Be willing to receive from everyone that the Lord may send to you to help prepare you for this different, exciting, fresh, and anointed church." You see, I was learning firsthand the importance of surrendering a church to the loving leadership of God.

We had been talking for two hours when Andrew finally asked, "What is that noise I hear in the background?" I apologized and explained that I was cooking as we talked. Since tomorrow was Thanksgiving and my family and I would be on a plane, I was cooking dinner today.

"You? Dr. Wanda Davis, *the Legend*, cook?" He seemed genuinely stunned and amused.

"Yes," I laughed. "I cook, wash, iron, and brush my own teeth!" He asked, so I rattled off my Thanksgiving menu: turkey, dressing, greens, yam casserole, potato salad, pies, cakes, and a special punch. He was just in shock. I think until that moment, he had only seen me as Dr. Davis, minister. Dr. Wanda, mommy, homemaker, chief cook and bottle washer caught him a little off guard. We laughed about that for a little while, then decided to hang up, both of us looking forward to our appointment in January. Before saying good-bye, I impulsively asked Andrew if he would stay over and preach that Sunday at my church. He hesitated, then quietly accepted.

Once the phone was returned to its cradle, misgivings haunted me. I had never heard this man preach, and I just turned over a Sunday service to him. I beat myself up for a minute, then sheepishly called Bishop Weeks, his pastor. After some conversation "around the bush," I tiptoed up on my reason for calling. I told him I had asked Andrew to speak at First Apostolic. "Uh…can he preach?" I asked casually. "Can he preach? Can he preach? The man's a preaching machine!" Bishop Weeks assured me that Andrew Turner's ministry would be a great blessing to my church. I hung up the phone, feeling much better, but still a little uneasy in my spirit. I think even that afternoon, I began sensing change in the air…

I set my apprehension aside in favor of thoughts about my upcoming holiday plans, and I finished preparing my meal. Even though it was our first Thanksgiving without Wayne, we managed to enjoy the delicious food and complemented it with lots of laughter. I think we were all anticipating the following morning. We would be leaving for the airport immediately following our annual Thanksgiving service. I and my children and a gentleman friend were going. My youngest daughter Whitney and her husband Timothy complained of sore throats and low-grade fevers, but we prayed for them, determined not to let anything keep us from our much-needed vacation.

I had just said goodnight to Whitney and her husband when the phone rang. It was my friend calling to tell me he didn't think he would be going with my family and myself to Hawaii after all. My heart dropped. "Lord, just when I think I'm ready to embrace change!" I was devastated, but I forced myself to remember that all things work together for good. I found my missing smile, put it back in place, and finished packing. I wasn't going to let a couple of sore throats keep us from enjoying ourselves, so neither would I let my bruised heart.

When I told my daughters about the change of plans, they tried to reassure me. "Don't worry, Mom. God has new friends for you to meet, maybe right in Hawaii." I appreciated their efforts, but I didn't want any more "new friends." Making new friends is difficult for me. I wanted something familiar, something comfortable. Yes, again I was struggling with celebrating change. But this time, I would not struggle long. I picked up a magazine that day and thumbed through it. "To resist change," one article pronounced, "is to resist life, like trying to swim against the current. When we accept change—and encourage it—we are in the flow of life."

When I saw that, I realized change is not an option. It's a necessity. It is change that processes a sinner to the righteousness of God. Paul said that if any man is in Christ Jesus, he is a new creature; old things are passed away and all things become new (see 2 Cor. 5:17). Imagine that. Without change, there would not be one righteous among us. Without change, there would be no leader to follow, no healing for sickness, no wealth to replace poverty. Sadness would never find joy without change.

Without change everything would remain the same. We would be fallen; the wages of our sin would still be owed.

Change is that difference that brings one into destiny. How can we get where we want to go if we aren't willing to change from where we are? How will we ever see the future if we are determined to live in the past? John F. Kennedy said, "Change is the law of life. And those who look only to the past or present are certain to miss the future." I would not miss mine. I was determined to stay on this track that embraced change.

I got back from Hawaii and shortly thereafter departed for the Holy Land as planned. When I returned, I continued to see my friend. There were no hard feelings about him missing our trip, and I really enjoyed his company. He was a wonderful, kind, gentle man, and I respected him.

Then some weeks later, one Monday morning, the Lord woke me up with instructions to end the relationship. I remember sitting straight up in bed and thinking that couldn't be God speaking to me. This man and I prayed together, worshiped together, challenged each other intellectually, supported each other. Why would I need to discontinue this relationship? Besides, we were not engaged, not even close. What if I went to him and said, "God told me to break it off with you," and he said, "Break what off?" I was not ready for that kind of embarrassment.

I love the humor of the Lord Jesus. As I sat there ruminating, the phone rang. It was a brother in Christ, Dr. Donald Wright, calling from North Carolina. He said, "The Lord spoke to me about you this morning. He has given you a hard thing to do today, but you'd better obey. Your blessings depend on your obedience." Once I got over the initial shock, I was furious. But I'm not stupid. I feared God and respected Dr. Wright as a man of God, so I obeyed.

I called my friend. Tears made their way silently down my face as I asked to see him for a few minutes that morning. Somehow God gave me the strength and courage to get through that morning. I met with my friend and shared with him what God had spoken into my heart about our relationship. When all was said and done, I remember returning to my car

48

with a heavy heart. This man was a special friend, someone I shared secrets with, someone who knew and understood some of my deepest fears. He had been there for me during some real tough times, and God was saying to end it.

I stopped by my office after that meeting. Much later my staff would tell me I looked so horrible that day that they were afraid to speak or approach me. I pretended to work for a few minutes, then went home and got back into bed. I lay there, unable to do much more than that. Then the phone rang. My sister Doris called to tell me that the Lord had shared with her that I was struggling with a difficult assignment and that she was to encourage me in my obedience and watch Him work a miracle. I recounted my struggle to her. She added grace and wisdom to my understanding and gave me some follow-up advice that would hasten the healing process for me.

Looking back, I see clearly the loving-kindness of a God who tenderly walked me through my pain. Every word of encouragement or exhortation was from Him. He knew I was hurting. There's a song lyric that says, "I hurt for you. I feel your pain. Your tears rolled down and left a stain, upon my heart. You're not alone. I've suffered too. I felt every trial that you've gone through from the start...."[1] I imagine that is the reality of His relationship with us. But as I gently rolled over in bed and wept, it was difficult to see that He was doing what was best for me. The pain of change had hit my heart.

The phone rang again. I was distantly aware that God was walking me through this process and was sending word to me through those who cared about me. This time the call was from New York. It was my dear friend and sister in Christ, Dr. Phyllis Carter. She had exciting news for me. She had been praying, and the Lord Jesus allowed her to see me rolled up in a fetal position, weeping. That was not exciting or news to me, but she quickly clarified. She said, "Wipe your eyes, because God says joy is coming your way soon!" And as if to punctuate His Holy Ghost telegram, I felt an overwhelming desire to rejoice that could have

---

1. Oleta Adams, "When Love Comes to the Rescue" (Evolution).

come only from Him. Wow! I jumped up and floated around my bedroom like a ballet dancer.

I was still on the clouds when the phone rang yet again. I was ready to hear just about anything at this point. It was Phyllis again. "Wanda, I'm sorry," she said. "What I told you wasn't exactly right." All right, I was ready to hear anything but *that*. Phyllis sensed my trepidation and laughed. "No, what God said exactly was 'joy was coming *this week*.' I was afraid to be that specific." Relieved, we both laughed and praised God, with two thousand miles between us, celebrating my coming change.

Change is not always pleasant at first, but through the unpleasantness, through the wilderness, we see the faithfulness of Jehovah at its most brilliant. I think of the children of Israel in their wilderness. God gave them manna and quail to eat. He made water come from a rock to quench their thirst. He had already parted the Red Sea for them and defeated their enemies. They just needed to believe He would lead them to the land that He had promised them.

In many wildernesses, we are given the manna of God's Word to sustain us. In our rockiest places, our thirst is sated by a kind gesture from a friend. There are those who go to war in the spirit realm on our behalf and deliver messages to us from the throne. Be grateful for every wilderness you find yourself in. The glory of God is so close in those times. He leads, protects, pushes, feeds, and comforts us in the wilderness. The greatest gifts of His presence are found in our greatest tribulation. That is why we are to count it joy when we fall into them.

Phyllis had said joy would come to me that week, the same week I had yielded my will to change because God said change. Well, guess what week it was. Remember Andrew C. Turner II? He arrived Thursday, just three days after that awful Monday morning. I couldn't see him the night he got in. I was down with a cold. Friday I rested all day, and Friday night I attended a church opening celebration for one of my "sons" in the gospel. But early Saturday morning, the Lord spoke clearly to me and advised me not to procrastinate another day. *Call Andrew Turner and schedule a lunch appointment*, was His mandate. I was still smarting

50

from the last order He'd given, and I was tired and fighting a cold. If the truth be told, I was fighting God, but I'm sure He was quite unimpressed with my puny efforts at combat.

I was to dismiss my security and driver and pick up Elder Turner personally. I was to be more than "presentable," get my hair done, and take him to lunch. I was a nervous wreck. I was not used to meeting so informally people I didn't know. I had forgotten about our comfortable conversation. That didn't count. We were on the phone. I felt so exposed and unprotected, and I didn't know why. I prayed silently as I obeyed and was reminded that God was with me, guiding and guarding me, every step of the way. So I called Elder Turner and apologized for the two-day postponement of our meeting and invited him to lunch.

I picked him up from his hotel. When he got in my car, a gentle, peaceful spirit of quiet courtesy entered with him. I was still a little nervous. I informed him that I only had two hours for our meeting. He smiled very politely and never even reminded me that he had already waited two days for this appointment. He just said he was glad my cold was better. His calm demeanor totally disarmed me. In a few minutes, we were as we were on the phone that evening months ago. We talked about our lives, our ministries, our families, our former mates, and our dreams for the future.

Before I knew it, two hours had stretched to six. We sat through lunch, brunch, and early dinner before we realized how late it was getting. Then he looked up and asked, "Would you like to go with me to Disneyland?" Disneyland? *Maybe you're not clear on who you're speaking to. I'm a pastor. I'm an evangelist. I am a CEO. A very busy woman with appointments and security and a staff of people I'm responsible for. I don't have time for Mickey and Minnie!* All those thoughts ran through me, but when it came out of my mouth it sounded like, "Yes! I would love to go to Disneyland!" The thought of just playing and enjoying myself suddenly appealed to me a lot. It had been so long.

I rushed home to change. I remembered as I pulled up that there was a bridal shower being held at my home that day for one of our church members. Some of the guests were still there when I ran in. I ran upstairs to change and left Andrew downstairs with them. Nobody said anything, but you could see questions on everybody's face. *"Who's that with Sister Wanda?" "Where does she know him from?" "Where has she been all day?" "Where is she going now?"* On and on the questions silently decorated the faces of everyone there until I was changed and on my way to Disneyland. Elder Turner seemed to be absolutely amused by it all.

When we got to Disneyland, Andrew asked me to get on a roller coaster with him. I had not been on a roller coaster in almost 20 years. I have a very sensitive stomach, and I had gotten sick. For some reason I didn't want him to know that, so I just told him no, I did not ride roller coasters and hadn't for a long time. I tried to put enough force behind it so as not to encourage any further discussion. He just smiled that gentle, kind smile and said, "Didn't you just tell me that God gave you and your church the order to 'celebrate change' this year? Well, you are with Andrew. *Change* and ride the roller coaster."

I remember walking with him to the log ride first and silently pleading with God that if I had ever done anything to please Him in life, could He not let me lose my lunch in front of this man. God must have heard my prayer, because I did fine on the log ride. Then Andrew said, "Oh look, there's the Matterhorn. Let's try that." I looked up at that mountain and prayed again.

As the attendant strapped me into my seat, I felt tears falling from my eyes. Andrew was behind me and didn't know that I was crying. He wouldn't have understood anyway. I didn't understand. I asked God, "Lord, what is happening to me? What is making this night so different, and why am I crying?" He spoke gently, but clearly to my heart. "You know what is happening. I am placing love in your heart for this man."

Love? I was afraid to believe it. I know what I heard, but could it really be? I think I was so shocked that I forgot to be scared on the Matterhorn. We finished that ride and sat for what seemed like hours, sipping hot chocolate, laughing, sharing, and laughing some more. On the way back to the parking lot, Andrew bought me balloons. To me they represented my "celebration" of change. I still have those balloons. Of course the air has gone out of them, but I keep them as a reminder that what God promises, He brings to pass.

The next morning, during worship service, our choir sang a new song and dedicated it to me. The song was titled "Lonely Days Are Gone." They could not have known how perfect and on time they were. They were rehearsing it before I had left my other relationship, before I met Andrew, before I fell in love with him. I began to weep. And it was as though a dam burst. All the tears I had not cried when Wayne was sick, when he died, when I was lonely and still had to serve my children and my church, erupted. I released my loneliness and fear. Most of all, I experienced the cleansing and healing that washes over us when we are faced with the glory of the faithfulness of God. And as every sad and dark place in me was emptied of its store of sorrow, I was filled with the bright newness of joy that comes in the morning.

When the choir finished singing, I introduced our guest speaker for the day, Reverend Andrew C. Turner II. His sermon was "God's Delays Are Not God's Denials." Believe me when I tell you that man preached, preached, preached, *preached*! And I wept again, this time with reverence, awe, and gratitude.

That afternoon some of the elders and deacons took Andrew to dinner. I stopped by and had an iced tea with them. I couldn't stay because I had a previous engagement at First Church of God. I instructed my staff and driver to put themselves at Reverend Turner's disposal. I did not know that he would ask them to bring him to the service I was attending.

The room was packed, but when he entered, I knew it. I felt his presence. My feeling was confirmed when, without special directions from anyone, the ushers brought Andrew from the last pew to the front row! As he was being seated, Bishop Benjamin Reid, my father in the ministry and pastor of First Church, leaned over and tapped me. He whispered, "Who is that young man? After church, bring him to my office, please." I wanted to ask why. I wanted to run after the benediction. But when I

53

looked around after the service, there was Andrew Turner walking toward Bishop Reid's office with my driver.

When I entered the office, Bishop Reid smiled at me and walked over to Andrew. Then, without warning, he literally slapped him in the forehead, and with a big, generous smile, he said, "You are special to God!" Then he turned to me and said simply, "I like him." I was mortified. I hadn't spoken to anyone about Andrew. And I didn't want him to think that I had told Bishop Reid anything. I just stood there, red as a beet, and left as soon as I could. The rest of the evening was like a dream.

We stopped by my house so I could change. My favorite aunt Janie was there; her opinion was very important to me. She liked Andrew right away. They chatted while I changed. When I came downstairs, Andrew was speechless. I was wearing a very elegant but casual cream and gold suit. I didn't know until later that cream and gold were special colors to him. (Needless to say, the very next week I had my secretary, who loved to shop, go out and buy me everything in cream and gold.)

We decided to go to the movies. I told him I was a little sleepy and not to take it personally if I nodded off during the movie. It would not be a reflection on him. He replied that if I went to sleep, he would consider it an honor, because he had heard that I only slept around people I trusted. He was right. I could fly ten to twelve hours and not sleep if I was sitting next to someone on the plane whom I didn't know or trust. And I was also known to drop off to sleep in a minute if I was with someone I was comfortable with.

To no one's surprise, I nodded off in the movie. When Andrew noticed, he encouraged me to rest and promised to tell me what happened later. Then he gently slid his hand into my hand and continued to watch the film. Sleep was forgotten completely as my toes literally curled when he touched me. My Lord, what was going on?

We left the theater, and I took him back to his hotel so he could pack and head for the airport. We talked for a few minutes, both of us acknowledging that God had birthed the miracle of relationship between us. It was both exciting and frightening. I left him in the hotel lobby entrance and drove home, a very different woman from the one he met a little over 24 hours earlier.

He called me from the airport before his flight was to leave, and he wrote to me on the plane and faxed it to my home the next morning. We talked several times during the day. In fact, we talked until the battery in his phone gave out.

On Tuesday evening, I taught a Bible study. The subject for the evening was "Love Is a Decision." I ministered and was ministered to. When I returned home, there was a wedding invitation from a young lady from our church in my mail. On the front was a poem titled, "How Will I Know When?" As I read it, I began to cry again. Also in the mail was a plaque about love and commitment from my pen pal in Atlanta, Joyce Hariston. And later that evening, I received a gift from one of the families at church. It was a beautiful negligee. The card said when they saw it, it reminded them of me and they felt I would need it "really soon."

The phone rang late that night. I trembled as I answered. It was Andrew. We confessed our belief that God had brought us together in love. Two days later, he called again. This time it was to ask me to marry him.

Change Your Mind

"Letting go" is an inescapable component of change. Sometimes I think it's the letting go that is the biggest problem for many of us, especially if we don't know what's in store. Often God will ask us to let go of something without telling us what's on the other side of His request. And we'll try to move forward and still hold on to what we're supposed to be releasing. It doesn't work. It's like attaching ourselves to something (or someone) with a rubber band. When God tells us to move, we do, but our heart isn't in it. So we stretch the rubber band until one of two things happens. We snap back into that old relationship, or habit, or sin. Or the rubber band breaks, and anyone who has had that happen knows that's always very painful.

1.   What item, person, habit, or problem are you holding on to that you know you should let go of?

2.   What is the worst thing that could happen if you let go?

3.   What is the best thing that could happen if you let go?

4. Read Luke 18:28-30 to know what Jesus says to us about letting go.

5. Part of letting go involves releasing your concerns about something and trusting God to handle it. Scripture tells us that God gives us the power to will and to do. Think about that. If you don't want to let go and welcome change, God can give you the power to want to. Read Philippians 2:13 and First Peter 5:6-7. Then go back to questions 1 and 2 and pray that God will give you the will to let go, then show you the way to let go. Then confide all your fears to Him and release them.

"Once upon a time there was a woman named Wanda Ann who lived in California with her two daughters Wendy and Whitney and their husbands Steven and Timothy and one grandson Steven Wayne..."

Change

Chapter Four

New What?

And I will bring the blind by a way that they knew not; I will lead them in paths that they have not known: I will make darkness light before them, and crooked things straight. These things will I do unto them, and not forsake them.

—Isaiah 42:16

"To fear love is to fear life, and those who fear life are already three parts dead."

—Bertrand Russell

"Fear knocked at the door. Faith answered. No one was there."

—Hind's Head Hotel, Bray, England
(on the front of the ancient mantel)

Andrew Turner had just proposed to me over the telephone. *There it was*, I thought, staring at the phone, the call long ended. The change I had looked forward to, had believed God for, was finally here. So why wasn't I celebrating? I loved this man. His gentleness and patience with me were almost too hard to believe. My heart had waited for this kind of love, had yearned for it. But I had known him for less than a week. My mind was well aware that the entire universe was framed in the same

61

amount of time. My mind understood that God could change the hearts of kings and princes in a matter of minutes. My mind had long ago grasped the notion that God guided and guarded the hearts of those who trusted Him. And I trusted Him. Didn't I? It was a time for serious reflection, prayer, and soul-searching.

The next morning, I woke early to attend a 5 a.m. prayer meeting. I slipped a Bible off the shelf to take with me. I almost dropped it as I pulled it down, and it fell open in my hands at Psalm 65. I had marked verse 4, which reads, "Blessed is the man whom Thou choosest, and causest to approach unto Thee, that he may dwell in Thy courts: we shall be satisfied with the goodness of Thy house, even of Thy holy temple." It was so amazing. God had given me this verse more than 12 years ago. I had made a note of the date. I remember at the time that it seemed strange and inappropriate.

That morning at prayer, the Lord whispered to me, "Wanda, be careful who you marry, for I must bless whomever you choose—not because of them, but because of My promise to you." I knew that I wanted to make sure I married a special man, an anointed man who loved Jesus. I certainly didn't want God to have to bless a deceitful, cunning, evil, or downright ungodly man.

I thought for a moment about the Scripture that says a man who finds a wife finds a good thing and gets favor from the Lord (see Prov. 18:22). Couldn't Andrew just "find" me without my having to think so hard about everything? Of course, then I wouldn't have to bother to seek God, would I? Where's the faith in that process? No, men do "find" wives, but women also must "choose" their husbands. We as precious, special, chosen women of God do not have to choose every man who finds us. We have a lot to say about whom we marry. And I wanted to make a wise choice. I wanted to acknowledge God in all my ways, including this one, so He could direct my path.

When we decide to accept and embrace change in our lives, according to the will of God, we are met with an immediate sense of peace. That peace is our indication that we have stopped struggling with God and that

He has let us know we're on the right track. If you take nothing else from this work, take this: Always follow your peace.

I should tell you here that peace and quiet are not the same thing, any more than solitude and loneliness are, or happiness and joy. Happiness is a state of well-being that has to do with what's "happening" in your life. Joy is that unspeakable understanding that all is well, no matter what is happening. Loneliness is the sadness that overcomes one who wishes he or she was not alone. Solitude is that "aloneness" that we seek out in order to find out who we are in God. And quiet is no more than a lack of audible noise. Peace, on the other hand, is the absence of all unnecessary internal "noise." It is that gift that makes the voice of God ring clearly in us.

Peace is the chief ally of effective change. And it is the first thing the enemy will try to disrupt when you are trying to make changes in your life. His assignment is to throw as much "noise" at you as he can to distract you from the right choice and steer you toward the wrong one. I thought that all my battles would end when I decided to embrace the changes God had in store for me. But I quickly realized that between "deciding" and "doing," there was a whole new series of encounters with satan to deal with. In other words, first there are the challenges *to* change. Then there are the challenges *of* the change. It makes sense. Any decision you make in obedience to God will bring you closer to Him. So naturally the devil is going to try to blow you off course.

Uncertainty is usually satan's first strike against the saint who is willing to change. If he can get you to second-guess yourself, to vacillate between options that once seemed to be distinct, he may be able to short-circuit your destiny. I began to question the logic of what I was considering. I was a grown woman with responsibilities, obligations, and commitments, and here I was acting like a silly schoolgirl. Children fall head over heels. Mature women keep their feet on the ground.

I earnestly and sincerely sought the Lord. I sought the wise counsel of men and women in the Body of Christ, including my own parents Bishop Lewis and Mary Stallworth, as well. God had placed so many special people in my life who assisted me in reaching a decision. One of them, my friend Dr. Betty Showell Tyson, called me from Indianapolis. She would call from time to time just to chat and often ended up counseling me about this thing or that.

Her calls had become more frequent since I had become a widow, but on this particular evening, she was calling to tell me that she knew a wonderful Christian man she wanted to introduce me to. He was a doctor she knew, and she thought we would enjoy each other's company. She wanted to arrange a lunch or a dinner for the two of us to meet.

I remember laughing and telling her that I had just met a man who had literally swept me off my feet. I told her I was in the process of praying about his proposal of marriage. She didn't seem surprised at all when I told her that I hadn't known this man for a week before he had proposed. (I hadn't told her who he was yet.) I realized the reason for her calm when she began to share with me the wonderful love testimony of her own courtship with her husband, Bishop James Tyson. She encouraged me to follow my heart and to seek the will of God concerning this new relationship.

Then, as if sensing my thoughts, she stressed that I was not to be concerned about public opinion. She and Bishop Tyson had met soon after he had lost his first wife. And after what seemed like a whirlwind courtship, they had a most beautiful wedding. The timing and circumstances surrounding their new love was not understood or accepted by everyone. Even some members of their families objected. But she told me, "Wanda, with all the pain, stress, and discomfort our decision caused, if I had it to do all over again, I would do what I did, exactly the way I did it!" She blessed me. I knew her well, and I knew for a fact that her marriage to Bishop Tyson was wonderful and special. God had truly blessed their union up until her death in 1997.

Betty's was not a logical marriage. And yet I could vouch for God's presence in it. My relationship with Andrew didn't really make sense. But I believed God was in it. I wondered, though, if that was just my desire speaking. I talked about it to my dear friend and brother Dr. Donald

Wright. He assured me that God was well aware of my thoughts, my feelings, and my desires. In fact, he emphatically reminded me, God could and would fulfill the desires of my heart, since He was the one who put them there in the first place! (See Psalm 37.) The question was not whether or not it is right to desire a new love and a new marriage. The question was whether or not Andrew C. Turner II is God's choice to fill that desire.

God knows that every change He seeks to make in our lives will be met with opposition from the enemy. Satan will try to cloud your mind by distracting you from the real issues at hand. He will try to throw carefully crafted logic in the face of a word of prophecy you may have received, or try to nullify a Scripture you read during your prayer time and were certain that it was God speaking to your spirit.

I don't care how big your Bible is; you will forget sometimes what the Word of God says about you and to you. That's why one of the items in the Holy Spirit's job description is to bring things to your remembrance. And He will do that sometimes by putting you before wise counselors, people who know you and know God's Word.

One of the worst things you can do in uncertain times is isolate yourself from counsel. If you're not sure who to go to, James tells us to ask God for wisdom and He will send it down in buckets, no questions asked (see Jas. 1:5-6). Wisdom nullifies uncertainty. It gives us clarity and makes sense according to the mind of God. Earthly rationale only takes into account what we see. That's why we are faced with so much uncertainty when we lean to our own understanding. Facts don't always mix with faith. The heart of God often contradicts the mind of men. That's why He so often moves us "beyond the expectations of men."

Once uncertainty is dealt with by our petition for wisdom, the devil pulls out his next weapon, which is fear. I remember asking the Lord to show me the "real" Andrew C. Turner. He led me to a study of David. He said that if I wished to know this man, to look at David the shepherd boy, the skilled archer and giant slayer, the praiser, the armor bearer, the warrior, and finally, He encouraged me to take a look at David the king.

Wow! What a study that was. I learned so much about Andrew. He was a lot like David. And I loved God so much that I knew it would be detrimental for me to marry anyone who did not also love and worship Him.

I also knew that my husband would need to understand the call of God on my life to praise, pray, worship, teach, and preach. I had asked the Lord to send someone who would respect the men and women who were already in my life. I have always had more male friends than female, and I didn't want to marry a jealous, outrageous nut.

The more I thought about it, the taller my order seemed to me. And the more I thought about Andrew, the more I realized what marriage would mean. This would be a union of tremendous change and transition. Andrew was gifted and anointed, and he had a powerful call of God on his life. We would not be a "normal little married couple." There were so many dynamics to consider. This would be a unique relationship that would combine ministry and business, East and West coast residences, two families of children (five adults, one child, and one grandchild), complicated financial systems, and on and on. The list grew.

I had so much to think about. Andrew and I would have to recognize the impact our former spouses—one living and one deceased—would have on our lives as we transitioned into our new "oneness" as a married couple. We both would have to embrace change to enter into the covenant of marriage. We would have to be willing to "remember not the former things, neither consider the things of old" (see Is. 43:18) if we were to embrace this "new thing" that God wanted to do in our lives.

Then I realized something. I had moved from considering "me" to considering "we." As fearful as I was about the complications of our being together, I loved him and could not imagine us apart. In that moment, my head and my heart were in one accord, and I knew in my spirit that God had worked to make it that way.

So on Saturday, exactly one week after we had met for lunch, I said yes to Andrew Carnegie Turner II.

Now What?

In the moment I agreed to become Mrs. Andrew Turner, God gave me peace. I began to see that He really had made a way in the wilderness and rivers in the desert for me. He didn't say He would make a puddle in the desert. His Word promises rivers—large, running streams, wide and flowing into bays, gulfs, seas, and even oceans. When we follow God on the path to change, we have access to the rivers and everything they flow into. In other words, God will begin to connect you to people, places, and things that will bless you because of your obedience to Him.

Isaiah 43 reminds us that when we change because God asks us to, He will take care of us. Remember the children of Israel. When they agreed to follow Moses out of Egypt, God honored their obedience by parting the Red Sea and providing a path for them to escape their painful past. Then He rained manna from Heaven and allowed water to flow from a rock to sate their thirst. When we embrace change according to the will of God, He obligates Himself to watch over us as we make the transition.

As wonderful as submitting to change can be, trust me, everyone will not be happy about it. If satan can't get you to reject change with uncertainty or fear, that doesn't mean he gives up. "Happily ever after" does not happen because he's been thwarted in his efforts to derail you. In reality, his attacks become more obvious at this point. But don't be fooled just because you can see them. For what his weapons lack in stealth, they make up for in their ability to inflict pain.

When my engagement was announced, I realized the only thing that had happened faster than our getting together was the spreading of the gossip about it. I was not unacquainted with being the topic of whispered conversation. Still, it hurt when one woman stated very bluntly that she didn't understand "why God would bless Wanda to marry two times and some of us have never experienced love or marriage the first time." I certainly didn't cancel my wedding to accommodate that woman's jealousy. But I will admit, there were many times in my solitude when I thought of special, beautiful, wonderful Christian women who desired marriage and family—and who were still single. I would pray for them and ask, "Lord, why have You so highly favored me?"

Part of my answer came four years later during a conversation with Terri McFadden, a friend and a gifted author and speaker. She pointed out that my life in Christ—my abundant life of blessings and miracles—stimulated some jealousy and even hatred among my enemies. And when they began to rise up, God blessed and favored me even more because of them. You see, He had to "prepare a table before me" in their presence. In truth, I have my enemies to thank for some of my blessedness.

When enemies show themselves to you through overt confrontation or covert gossip, your first instinct may be to fight back. Don't give in to it. God says in Isaiah 54:17 that no weapon formed against you will prosper and that every tongue that rises up against you in judgment you shall condemn. That doesn't mean that you will execute vengeance; that's God's job. It means that everything they have said about you to judge you will be condemned by the truth that God allows to shine forth in your life. People may say you don't deserve to be blessed, but when God pours out His favor on you, they will be found guilty as liars. But if you launch your own attacks and try to vindicate yourself, then you yourself will be guilty of the sin of pride. Satan will have successfully knocked you out of God's will.

Sin is the most obvious weapon he uses against us to short-circuit our efforts to reach our destiny. If he can't make you sin by stooping to the level of your enemies, he'll use your own hidden lusts and desires and the people you love. Proverbs 14:12 says, "There is a way which seemeth right unto a man, but the end thereof are the ways of death." I had been celibate for more than two and a half years when I became engaged to Andrew. We soon realized that we had the passion of 20-year-olds, but they were locked up in the responsibilities of 40-year-olds.

I remember traveling to New Jersey from California to meet Andrew's daughters Aneicka and Andrea. I had not seen Andrew for over a week, and it was so exciting to touch him, kiss him, hold hands, and gaze into his eyes, uninterrupted and not hindered by usual 3,000 miles that separated us.

One evening, after dinner with him and the girls, Andrew took me back to the hotel where I was staying. It had begun to rain, and I was feeling a little melancholy on the way. After seeing me safely to my room, Andrew went home. I was already missing him by the time he called to let me know he had made it home and to check on me. I began a game of seduction that was amazing. At the time, I didn't even realize that what I was doing was setting us up to violate the fidelity of our relationship with each other and with God.

I told him I was afraid of the rain, lonely, and a little frightened. I didn't have my daughters with me like he did. What was little ol' me going to do? Maybe he could come back to the hotel to keep me company. We both knew that wasn't a good idea, but I must admit, that wasn't in the front of my mind. I kept pushing. I remember Andrew telling me, "Wanda, you are placing us in an awkward position. If I don't come back the hotel, you will be upset. If I do return to see you, and things get out of hand, God is going to be upset." Looking back, that should have been enough to stop us both. But we talked, flirted, and talked some more. Then we hung up…because Andrew was on his way back to the hotel.

As he knocked at the door, the Holy Ghost spoke up one more time. "What do you think you're doing? If you push this, you will cancel every blessing on this relationship." It was the quickest cold shower I'd ever been fortunate enough to have. I marvel today at God's mercy. He didn't have to speak to me that one last time. He had already spoken. And I could not say I hadn't heard Him, first in my own spirit, and then through Andrew.

I opened the door and was immediately ashamed of myself. I told him I was sorry for pushing him to come back and begged his forgiveness. I knew that it was not the right time or place for us to consummate our love. In reality, we would not be consummating anything but our lust if things had gotten out of hand before we were married. After he left, I thanked God for delivering me from my own deceitful heart. At that moment, He showed me that there was a lot more than my virtue and Andrew's and my personal reputations at stake.

For more than 15 years I had been going all over the country and abroad preaching and teaching from my book *Sex Traps*. "No ringie, no dingie!" I had been declaring to hordes of single women struggling to live holy. And in just a few moments, I was about to violate the principles of righteousness that God had established in me and had called me to preach. As a married woman, I was faithful to one husband. As a widow, I was celibate. Now, just weeks before my wedding, satan was trying to set me up in the very trap I was teaching women to avoid. I thank God for Jesus, because through Him I am more than a conqueror. And with His wisdom, both Andrew and I decided we would ensure our victory as an engaged couple.

I made a decision not to return to New Jersey until I was married. For the duration of our engagement, our traveling was limited to meetings and conferences we attended or his trips to California, which were better supervised. I had the money, time, and desire to be with my fiancé every week, but I had to forego my desires in order to protect the victory I had been promised in the Word.

I was determined to walk down the aisle on my wedding day with no spot or wrinkle on my relationship. Was it difficult? Yes! Did I always want the victory? No! But thanks be to God who is definitely able to keep me (and you) from falling. When May 13th rolled around, I donned my wedding gown proudly and walked down the aisle with my daddy (and my heavenly Father) in total victory to join Andrew Turner in very holy matrimony.

When Andrew and I embraced God's will concerning our marriage, we were blessed in so many areas. Our home in Los Angeles was reconstructed and redecorated. The mayor of Inglewood at that time, Edward Vincent, honored us by allowing us to have our wedding reception at the city's new Racetrack Pavilion. Friends blessed us with our wedding cake, our reception, and so much more.

Now that I was married and my decision to change made, do you think satan was through with me? Of course not. (Settle it now, child of God. He won't be through with you until God is through with him, and not a moment sooner.) When uncertainty, fear, and temptation to sin have struck out and you have embraced change, there is yet another tactic left: discord and discontent.

I expected the early months of my new marriage to be a season of adjustment. But it's amazing how easily adjustment can become doubt. We think that when we follow God that everything will be perfect and wonderful, like pages from a fairy tale. But remember that the rivers that are flowing are still in the wilderness. There are still challenges to overcome. And during the process of "overcoming," satan will try to shift your focus. God wants you to remember the beauty of the wilderness, the joy and the provision. But one spat, one thing left out of order, will pull your focus to all the things that are wrong with your circumstances. Your joy is diminished and you begin to wonder if you've made the right decision.

At that point doubt has crept in, and satan's goal in getting you to doubt the wisdom of your decision to change is twofold. First, he wants you to doubt God and therefore not seek His help. Secondly, he wants you to make a decision to undo your change without consulting God. Instead of celebrating change, he wants you to question it and abandon it. That way he can celebrate when you change your mind and miss your blessing.

There's an old prayer that asks, "God grant me the serenity [peaceful spirit] to accept the things I cannot change, the courage to change those I can, and the wisdom to know the difference." I don't believe we have any power within ourselves to change anything, so my prayer is slightly different. My prayer is, "Lord, grant me the serenity to be still for You when I'd rather move, the courage to move for You when I'd rather be still, and the wisdom to know the difference."

I remember sharing the pain of change and adjustment in my newlywed season with Dr. Bam Crawford. Fear and doubt were plaguing me. Often I would become distracted by people and their opinions when my decision to change my life brought discomfort to them. "What if we did miss God and His timing?" I asked her. She told me simply, "You cannot go back and undo anything that has already been done. You cannot let people continue to judge what you believe to be the will of God for your life. You must forget those things behind you and press." *Where had I heard that before?*

I had wished that everyone would be as happy about my decision as I was when I made it. Sometimes I wished *I* could be as happy about it all the time. But there was so much upheaval. It was difficult to hold on to my peace. I had to realize that change is not always easy. In fact, it usually isn't. If it were, I wouldn't be writing this book. I learned that the key to dealing with doubt and discontent is in focusing our attention on what we believe God said to us, not on the results of our response to what God said.

We cannot make decisions based on their positive outcomes. If we did, we would have to undo anything that resulted in our discomfort or unhappiness. That's the way the world does things. The world says it's all right to leave a marriage because one or both spouses simply aren't happy. The world says we should be able to pursue anything that makes us happy, sex without marriage, marriage to someone of the same gender, pornography, gossip, excessive drinking, etc. The world worships happiness. The child of God worships God and, as I said before, He gives joy.

As soon as we settle into our faith, without specific perimeters and with the confidence that God will reveal Himself in our choice to change, something miraculous happens. That decision that seemed so right, then wrong, then "maybe" right, becomes clear. And our own limited expectations are shattered and replaced by a glorious blessing that is exceedingly abundantly above all we asked or thought.

As I settled into my marriage with Andrew and forgot about everything except my promise to God to celebrate change no matter what, God blessed me beyond measure. I not only had been blessed with a kind, strong, praying man, but our church also was blessed with a new pastor, ready and willing to lead it into its destiny. With Bishop Andrew Turner installed as its new head, First Apostolic became New Bethel Apostolic Ministries, and World Won for Christ Ministries International became M.E.C.C.A., declaring its new vision as a Ministry of Excellence

Challenging Christians to Advance. You see, God had even bigger plans for our union than we did.

To many it seemed we had wed too soon. Some thought we were mismatched and that our marriage wouldn't last more than a year or two. Some were certain that we were completely out of the will of God. But I remembered my friend Dr. Betty's word about public opinion. And I remembered Bishop Donald's comforting words about God's desire to fulfill my desires. Most of all, though, I remembered God's word to me: "Blessed is the man whom Thou choosest...." I did choose this man, because I believed God had chosen him. So he would be blessed. And because we would become one, *we* would be blessed.

An old folktale, retold by Angela Elwell Hunt, illustrates the importance of celebrating change itself and not the unexpected results of it.

Once three young trees growing on a hill in the woods discussed their dreams. One wanted to be carved into a beautiful treasure chest and inlaid with precious gems. Another desired to become a large sailing ship, carrying mighty kings around the world. The third tree longed to grow straight and tall, so that when people looked at him they would think of God.

When the trees reached maturity, two were cut down, as they wished. However, the first was made into a feed box for animals, rather than a treasure chest. The second became a small fishing boat sailing a lake, rather than a mighty seafaring vessel. Against its wishes, the third tree also was cut down, taken from the woods, and its crude beams forgotten in a lumberyard.

Time passed and the trees forgot their dreams. Then one night a poor young couple came to a stable and laid their newborn baby in the hay of the feed box. The first tree sensed that he held the greatest treasure imaginable.

Later, the small fishing boat carried some men on the lake. A fierce storm tossed the small boat about mercilessly. One of the men, who had been sleeping, awakened, stood up and spoke to the storm. It stopped immediately! The second tree knew he was carrying the greatest king ever.

One Friday, some time after this, angry men pulled the third tree's forgotten beams from the pile in the lumberyard. They forced a man to carry them to the top of a hill, then nailed his hands and feet to them and placed the structure upright in the ground. The third tree was very, very sad.

Ms. Hunt ends her retelling of this classic story with these words:

"But on Sunday morning, when the sun rose and the earth trembled with joy beneath her, the third tree knew that God's love had changed everything.
"It had made the first tree beautiful.
"It had made the second tree strong.
"And every time people thought of the third tree, they would think of God.
"That was better than being the tallest tree in the world."[1]

I got everything I had prayed for, and more. I celebrate my marriage still. But it is not the only major change that occurred in my life. There are many others that were even harder to make. In the next chapter, we will talk about those changes that God has to force on us.

---

1. Angela Elwell Hunt, *The Tale of Three Trees* (Colorado Springs, CO: Lion Publishing, 1989), 25-26.

Change Your Mind

I often wonder why birds don't just stay in their eggs when they discover what a chore it is to get out of them. And butterflies experience great trauma as they exit their cocoons. So many of us experience great pain as we move from one chapter of our lives to the next. And unlike nature, we can choose not to make the change.

But we should learn the lessons nature teaches us. Birds leave their eggs and butterflies exit their cocoons because they have outgrown them. Moreover, the egg and the cocoon contain only enough food to keep them up to a certain size. Once they reach that stage in their development, they must embrace their new life or die. Have you outgrown some things or people in your life? Is it time for you to "fly" in your career or your ministry?

1. Track the progression of a major change you've made in your life. Write down where you were and the decision you had to make in order to change your circumstances.

2. Immediately following your decision to make the change, did you experience any uncertainty? How did you deal with it?

3.   What were your fears? How did you handle them?

4.   Were you tempted to get off track in any way? Did you experi-
     ence any guilt as a result of your decision, or any personal
     attacks?

5.   Are you content about the change? If not, why?

6.   What were the unexpected blessings that resulted from your
     decision to change?

"Once upon a time there was a man named Andrew Carnegie who lived in New Jersey…"

Change

Chapter Five

Complications

If thou faint in the day of adversity, thy strength is small.

—Proverbs 24:10

"O, do not pray for easy lives. Pray to be stronger men. Do not pray for tasks equal to your powers. Pray for powers equal to your task."

—Phillips Brooks

God loves us just the way we are…but He loves us too much to let us stay the way He found us. We must come to an understanding that we no longer belong to ourselves. When we were saved, we became a part of the blood-bought Body of Christ. So when change occurs in our lives, it occurs in much the same way it does in a human body.

Parts grow internally and in external appearance. They are acted upon and affected by their environment. They depend on other body parts to function properly. They impact other parts when they malfunction. They compensate when other parts malfunction. Can a foot function properly when a toe does not grow, develop, or change? Also, every part of the body is controlled by the head. Growth, development, maturation, and movement are directed by signals from the brain. In other words, all change is the responsibility of the brain.

Spiritually speaking, when we are saved, the Holy Spirit gives us "the mind of Christ," which takes over responsibility for how and when we change. And that change does not occur in a vacuum. Others are impacted and affected when we change. That's why there are times when we will not be asked to change. We will be *forced* to change for the sake of our growth and the benefit of others.

Complications are those painful, difficult things that God allows into your life at those junctures where change is not an option. It is mandatory, not just in its nature, but in its timing as well. Complications happen when God's sovereign plan reaches a "purpose point." The apostle John was exiled to the island of Patmos by an evil Roman emperor who took great joy in persecuting Christians. John was in his nineties at the time, and the imprisonment had to be difficult for him. But it was on that island that the Lord came to him and gave him the word we read today as the Book of Revelation. John could not choose to avoid that major change in his circumstances.

God's purpose points must be honored, so He doesn't leave them to us to see that they are. He causes complications to shape and direct our behavior, beliefs, and our biases. When Joseph found out that Mary was pregnant, he tried to make changes by divorcing her privately to spare her name and his shame. But God's plan was to have Joseph, who was descended from David, and Mary, who also was descended from David, marry and become the parents of Jesus. So God intervened, and Joseph had to endure all the gossip and embarrassment that surely took place when he took a pregnant woman as his wife.

We have purpose points in our lives too. They are signaled by complications. The important thing to know about complications is that their purpose is not to change our circumstances or our situation. Complications are specifically designed to change *us*. They are deliberately difficult, purposely painful, and intentionally intense. And we are never the same when we emerge from them. They are the tools of internal change.

Complications

When God introduces these complications into your life, it is a sure sign that He's doing intricate, spiritual microsurgery. These are the times when we are brought to our knees by tragedy, forced to raise our voice in praise "in spite of," and forced to drink from the well of our own tears to survive in the blistering heat of the desert. Complications make us wonder if God has left us or forsaken us. But complications are always, always, *always* God's way of drawing us to Himself.

Complications come in three types, each one designed for a specific purpose and requiring a different response from us. Though complications force change, our focus as we endure them should not be on the change, but on God, since the changing is totally out of our hands. The three types of complications—troubles, trials, and terrors—are the tools God uses to change us. Let's look at each of them more closely.

Trouble

We find ourselves faced with trouble when God is trying to move us from a place of disobedience to one of obedience. It's so easy to do what you feel like doing when you're not being punished for it. But God loves us too much to allow us to stay on a path that will surely lead to destruction. He would rather hurt you to put you back on the right path, so that you'll remember the pain the next time you think about straying.

Have you seen those wonderful paintings of Jesus as the Good Shepherd, carrying a little lamb on His shoulders? In actuality, you find shepherds carrying sheep in that manner when the sheep is prone to wander away from the flock. At first the shepherd will warn the lamb with his rod to try to steer him back to the flock. If that doesn't teach the little animal, the shepherd will sometimes break his leg, and while he's healing from this painful lesson, the shepherd has to carry him while he drives the rest of the flock. Jesus said that a good shepherd will leave 99 sheep to go find the one that is lost. And He loves us enough to find us and take steps to see that we don't get lost again.

For the child of God, trouble is the merciful hand of a loving Father brought down to correct before it comforts. Hebrews exhorts us not to hate the chastening of God. It's proof that He loves us. (See Hebrews 12.) My friend Bishop Kenneth Ulmer says when you're in the mall and you see somebody else's kids acting up, you don't go over and spank them. But you don't hesitate to take a belt to your own. He says that if you're in sin and nobody's spanking you, you might want to ask yourself whose child you are!

The purpose of trouble is simply to change our behavior. It's God's way of saying, "Stop that!" Trouble hurts. It's supposed to. How many of you give your child an ice cream cone when he acts up? The only right response to trouble is obedience. When you find yourself in trouble because of something you've done, or are even playing at doing, you need to obey, because disobedience puts you on a path away from God. And disobedience can only prepare you for another act of disobedience. Obedience does just the opposite. It brings you closer to God and prepares you for another act of obedience.

I used to complain that God had me on such a short leash. I would see other saints get away with stuff that I got punished for just thinking about. But when I see how much harder it is for them to get out of trouble, I'm content to keep my chain short.

I remember a time of testing when I became very lonely. I was a young wife married to a young man who was very ill. There were times when I literally craved male companionship. I wanted adult attention and conversation. I wanted someone to think I was beautiful, and say it. I wanted to see that look of admiration and appreciation that only a man can give a woman. My man was alive, but ill. He was alive, but he often suffered memory loss, an inability to express himself, and during the last four months of his life, had diminished vision. Many times I wanted someone to share my heartache with, to be with me as I lived through my challenges and crises. The one I shared my life with was himself in a crisis, facing challenges of his own.

While I was with my husband, I felt I had to be upbeat, positive, full of faith, and constantly interceding and declaring "all is well" when sometimes I just wanted to be held, comforted, and touched myself. I wanted to be allowed to cry, complain, and whine.

During this season, I had interactions with many men because of my ministry responsibilities. After all, most other pastors are men, and almost all my local church deacons and elders were men. But my pastoral relationships did not meet my need for natural, human companionship. So of course satan was standing nearby to set me up with a trap.

I met a kind, Spirit-filled man who became available to pray with me and for me, believe God with me for miracles, encourage me when I was discouraged, laugh with me, support me in down times, and challenge me always to believe God and His Word in spite of my circumstances. My conversations, in person and on the telephone, became increasingly more important to me. My day began with calls from or to this man. My afternoons were sustained with calls to or from this man. My nights were calmed with conversations to or from this man. Soon he became, I thought, too important to me. I was a married woman. I had taken vows to love, honor, and cherish. I had promised to forsake all others.

I was devastated to discover that I was, in a sense, "involved" with a man other than my husband, even if it was just conversation, time, and prayer. We were enjoying conversation after conversation, trading compliments, encouraging one another, and "noticing" one another. Since the gentleman was single, I would imagine what kind of relationship we would have if we were both available.

After a while, I realized that I needed wise counsel regarding this relationship. The line was blurring between friendship and temptation. I called two people I trusted. One, a man, reminded me that all love is from God and that as a mature, Christian woman, I should not necessarily reject the relationship, but recognize that God may have sent this special man to comfort and console me during this terrible time. The other, a girlfriend, said that God knew what I was going through and had sent a friend to bless me. Neither of those answers satisfied me completely. Neither of them addressed the troubling of my spirit.

Finally, I called a minister whom I regarded as my spiritual father. I shared my predicament with him and told him how uncomfortable I was with my new male friend. To my surprise he laughed and asked permission to share a testimony with me. He explained that about ten years prior, the Lord had put a special love and concern in his heart for a young couple in ministry. While he loved the husband of the couple, he had a special regard and love for the young wife. So much so, that he had discussed his feelings about her with his wife and daughters. He knew in his heart that God had divinely assigned him to walk with this young Christian couple, and this woman in particular.

I wondered who the couple was. As if I had spoken the question aloud, he asked me if I was ready to hear who that young lady was. After a moment's hesitation, he confirmed that I was the person whom God had placed special love and concern in his heart regarding.

I was shocked and amazed. Looking back over the years, I realized that not once had this kind, gentle, and loving man of God made me feel uncomfortable in our fellowship together. Not once had he compromised his relationship with God, his wife, or his family. He simply made himself available to me and at times would share that God had put me, my ministry, or our family on his heart for prayer. He showed special love and regard for my husband before, during, and after his illness.

We talked further, and he too explained that God would place special people in our lives for special times. But we have a responsibility to confer with God with respect to the guidelines for any relationship we encounter, particularly those that develop outside of our marriage or at a time when there is stress on the marriage. He advised me to know that I must *commit to obey, submit wholly to God*, and *honor the boundaries set by Him* regarding the relationship.

I realized I had not done that. I was responding to my own need without seeking God. I repented of that sin. It was so easy to focus on the changes or how I would adjust to them and not focus on God. Even the people I initially sought for counsel were addressing the situation and not the issue that brought the situation to me. I was alone and needed comfort, and I did not seek it in God and let Him guide me to someone. I was without a husband in that season, and I did not allow God to be that husband. The world would have told me I had done nothing wrong. But God knew that when He troubled my spirit, I would seek Him and find out that I was headed in the wrong direction. I was on my way to breaking my marriage vow to forsake all others.

I immediately sought the Lord about the boundaries of this new relationship. He gave me explicit instructions: 1) Do not initiate any phone calls to him for any reason. 2) Remove myself from locations, places, and people where I knew he would be. 3) Walk and talk discreetly at all times, and do not violate any part of my covenant with my spouse.

I wept over the instructions, but I was committed to complying with them. In return, God spoke quietly and assured me that if I walked in obedience to His will regarding this relationship "during all the days of my husband's life," that He would honor me, bless me, and change me from tears to smiles, from grief to gladness, from sorrow to joy.

So many days, so many times, it was difficult not to pick up the telephone and call my friend, but God and His Word would constrain me. Often I would be driving in my car, hurting, lonely, and alone…not knowing who I could call who would really understand. Almost automatically, my hands would reach out to the car cell phone and begin dialing numbers that I knew by heart (office, residence, pager…). Immediately the Spirit of God would caution me. *Don't call him.* In tears, I would delete the call to my friend and initiate one to God for strength, for help, and for advice. And He was always there, to give, to help, to love me.

Shortly after I received my instructions from God regarding my behavior as a married Christian woman in the company of single Christian men, my husband went home to be with the Lord. When he died, I was by his side, a wife who loved and honored him. When we find ourselves in trouble, the only response is to remain faithful to God and obedient to His instructions, no matter how grievous they may seem. We are more than conquerors through Christ, more than able to withstand anything satan sends our way to kill, steal, and destroy all that God has placed in us.

Many times, God will allow hardship to befall us that ushers us into change to prevent a greater catastrophe from happening. The scare of sudden chest pains may "encourage" us to be better stewards over our bodies and perhaps prevent a heart attack in the future. It's amazing how many of us don't take the responsibility of living a healthy lifestyle seriously. We expect Jesus to do it all.

We claim the healing power of God and would rather lay hands on somebody in the hospital than tell them to take their hands off that second helping of macaroni and cheese. We want to walk on in Jesus' name, but forget walking on that treadmill you just bought. We want to believe God for lower blood pressure without lowering the amount of time we spend working at the office.

Then God, in His infinite mercy, fires a warning shot. A mild heart attack, a stroke, an ulcer, and diabetes are often traceable to the sin of a poorly kept body. The pain and shock of such a diagnosis will usually propel us into change. We'll chew on fresh carrots and celery sticks until the rapture, if necessary. We'll quit that second job and suddenly have time for church, prayer meetings, Bible study, and the usher board.

An alcoholic or a drug addict may find themselves wrecked on the side of the road. That man or woman caught up in fornication may contract an STD. That unfaithful husband may come home to changed locks. God has a way of letting you know that He's through letting you slide. By the time He allows trouble to have its way with you, I promise you, He has already asked you to do right. Now He's telling you.

Jonah heard God tell him to go to Nineveh. He even knew what to say when he got there. But Jonah wasn't going to obey. In fact, he made a mad dash in the opposite direction toward Tarshish. He was hoping to go far enough away that God would change His mind and get another boy to do the job. But as you know, God let Jonah encounter a little trouble with some fellows on a boat who threw him overboard, where he was swallowed up by a great fish. To make a long story short, Jonah did commit to obey God. The Bible says once Jonah decided to obey, God spoke to the fish, and it vomited him up onto dry land.

Trouble is not God's final judgment against us. It does not last forever. God's goal when He allows it to strike us is to get us to obey. Jonah had brought all his troubles on himself. Yet, when he confessed, repented, and humbled himself to obey, God was merciful. One of the most wonderful changes God can develop in us is the change from disobedience to obedience. God is not up in Heaven waiting to punish us; He is waiting to bless us. Disobedience disqualifies us for many of His blessings. So sometimes He has to force us to obey so He can bless us. We are pitiful, aren't we?

Trials

We find ourselves faced with trials when God is testing our faith in Him. When our circumstances change drastically and we can't trace our new situation directly to our disobedience (in fact, it is often the result of obedience), it is a sure sign that we are being tested or tried. While the purpose of trouble is to change our behavior, the purpose of a trial is to change our mind. We are transformed (changed) by the renewing of our minds when we allow God to take us through a trial.

"Proving our faith" is a concept that many don't understand. Most of us see that and think that God is trying to see if we have faith, so He allows a test. In actuality, you can take that phrase at face value (or faith value). He allows trials to prove *that* we have a certain amount of faith. Before the trial, He knows you have what it takes to get through it. He just wants *you* to know that you have reached that level of faith in Him. There is a wonderful illustration of this principle found at the potter's wheel.

After a potter shapes a pot on a wheel, he puts it in the oven to harden the clay. Most people think that it is the heat from the fire that makes the pot firm. In reality, it is the shape of the pot *before* you put it into the fire that ensures it will keep its shape. If the pot was not formed correctly on the wheel, it won't stand up to the pressure of the heat. When God puts us in the fire, it is not until He is sure we've got what it takes to stand the heat. That's why God can promise us in His Word that He won't put any more on us than we can bear. In other words, He won't put us in the fire unless He knows we can take it.

Trials often, but not always, follow periods of great spiritual success or learning. We are often at a place where we feel very strong in our faith, very capable. You might encounter a trial right after you successfully began a much-needed ministry at your church. A new, Spirit-filled marriage may be tried, or even one that has reached a milestone or two. I often see new preachers and pastors excited about what God is doing with and through them when they minister. Their churches are growing at alarming rates. People are being blessed, healed, delivered, and comforted. It seems nothing can go wrong. And then...

Trials are probably harder to accept than trouble. At least with trouble, you know that you did something to bring it on. You can take responsibility. But trials often feel like you've been abandoned or wrongly attacked. In Isaiah 54:7-8 God declares, "For a small moment have I forsaken thee; but with great mercies will I gather thee. In a little wrath I hid My face from thee for a moment; but with everlasting kindness will I have mercy on thee, saith the Lord thy Redeemer." This is a tough word to hear when you've been doing all you know to do to obey and live right. It's tougher still when the trial you're facing involves the pain of a loved one.

Someone's cancer may become your trial. A loveless marriage may become a trial. A difficult in-law or a wayward child can be used by God as a trial in your life. Regardless of its source, you should know that trials are an inevitable component of the Christian life. Paul reminds us in Romans 8:17, "And [since we are] children, then heirs; heirs of God, and joint-heirs with Christ; if so be that we suffer with Him, that we may be also glorified together." Dear brother and sister, that means if we call ourselves children of God, we are heirs to the blessings of King's kids, but we cannot escape the suffering that goes along with that privileged designation.

Complications

Do you remember Job? When you look at Job 42:12, you'll find these words: "So the Lord blessed the latter end of Job more than his beginning: for he had fourteen thousand sheep, and six thousand camels, and a thousand yoke of oxen, and a thousand she asses." Verse 13 continues, "He had also seven sons and three daughters." We see a little earlier in verse 10 that "the Lord turned the captivity of Job, when he prayed for his friends: also the Lord gave Job twice as much as he had before."

Now wait a minute. Notice when the Lord gave Job twice as much: Job prayed for his friends, and the Lord *turned the captivity* of Job. What captivity? Well, way back in chapter 1 of Job, God gave satan permission to "trouble" Job, or put him through a trial. In other words, God gave satan permission to attack, assault, and rob Job, who, in Job 1:1 was declared "perfect and upright, and one that feared God, and [hated] evil."

Picture it. God and satan are having a discussion, and God says, "Have you considered My servant Job?" Then satan says, "Of course he fears You. You've blessed him and protected everything You've blessed him with. But if You took all that away, he'd curse You to Your face!" So the Lord told satan, "Take your best shot. Just don't kill him." Just as God said to Satan, "Have you considered My servant Job," He has also said, "Have you considered My servant Wanda, Andrew, Mary, Carol, Joyce, Phillip, John, Cory, Gayle, Whitney," and on and on...

Within hours of God's lifting the hedge from around Job, satan began to test him. His oxen and asses were stolen. His servants were killed. His sheep and their shepherds were consumed by fire. His camels and their caretakers were stolen and killed. His home was destroyed by a hurricane that also killed all his sons and daughters and everyone else in the household. Then, in the second wave of the trial, Job himself was stricken with sore boils from head to toe. He was tormented and taunted by his wife and judged by his friends. My Lord, Job rewrote the definition of affliction and captivity. But God was setting Job up for a change.

When the trial gets to Job, he complains to God. He cannot understand why he's being put through so much. So God answers his question with 74 questions of His own. By the time God is finished, Job repents of his audacity to question the Lord's sovereignty. And in Job 42:5 he says, "I have heard of Thee by the hearing of the ear: but now mine eye seeth Thee." Before his trial, Job's relationship with God was one of works only. He did what he was told to do. His behavior was upright and perfect. But he had not "seen" God. He didn't have a true understanding of just how "God" God is. The trial changed his mind and expanded his knowledge of the Lord from hearsay to personal experience.

When we encounter trouble, God expects us to obey. Trials require us to wait for direction or revelation. God is usually silent during a trial. He seems to be ignoring us as we cry, shout, and beg for some sign, any sign, to tell us what to do. But the purpose of a test in school is to prove what you already know. Would you raise your hand in class during a test and ask the teacher to tell you the answers? You know the answers. You just have to remember them. That's what the Holy Spirit is for. He's your spiritual memory bank. He's also your comfort. He'll tell you not to panic about the test and instead to ask yourself what you're being tested on. You're being tested on what you believe. And once you know what you believe, you can settle, if a little uncomfortably, into your situation until your change arrives. And it will arrive.

On the way to celebrating that change is a road called "patience" and a place called "time." James 1:4 declares, "But let patience have her perfect work, that ye may be perfect and entire, wanting nothing." Let your time of suffering complete, mature, and finish you so that you live with "no lack." That's why James tells us to rejoice when we find ourselves in the midst of a trial (see Jas. 1:2). It means a blessing is on the way. As we patiently suffer, allowing our trials to prepare us for change, God uses that time to work every part of that trial for our good. He wants to bless us. He wants to prosper us. He wants to provide for us. But many of us would abort our blessings if God did not prepare us to receive them first.

Think about a weight lifter. He doesn't start off lifting 300 pounds. He learns to lift progressively. Some of us can't handle the $25,000 salary we're making now, and we're asking God to bless us with millions.

90

So He has to test us and take what we already have to teach us how to appreciate it and be a good steward over it. Then He can bless us with more. As we handle what God gives us with wisdom, generosity, and gratitude, He gives us more to handle, in every area of our lives.

Let me just say here that the purpose of a trial is never to punish us; it is to make us better prepared for what God has prepared *for* us. Sometimes, though, it's hard to tell the difference between a trial and trouble when it's not happening to you. And if you're not careful, you'll find yourself judging somebody's trial as trouble, like Job's friends did. Or you'll find yourself trying to convince someone to avoid a trial because you couldn't imagine going through it yourself, like Job's wife. She knew that the trial would end if Job just cursed God. She attempted to abort Job's destiny. How much could you really love someone and suggest he do something that would cause him to be struck down by God? I don't think it was an accident that she is never mentioned by name.

We may not understand the trials and tests of relatives, friends, and spouses. But we should never allow satan to use us to bring more pain to them in their days of difficulty. When we do, we risk losing our place in God. Our very name can be blotted out of the Book of Life or, at the very least, we become unwitting tools of iniquity.

Terror

Terror is that complication that carries us to the very limits of our mind's ability to think, our body's ability to act, and our heart's ability to receive and express the love of God. Terror is described as a crisis of the soul; a time when we are facing something heretofore unknown and not experienced, and God is asking us to go through it anyway. When we face terror, we have met something we cannot think our way past or around. We can't change our circumstances to avoid it because God has ordered our every step to it and has left us no way of escape.

When God inflicts this agent of change, He is aware that you have never been down this particular path before. He leaves you open and vulnerable to the spirit of fear. When terror strikes, it is for the sole purpose of stretching the boundaries of your love for God and your ability to allow His perfect love to cast out fear.

First John 4:18 says that with fear comes "torment." That torment is the punishment inflicted by fear on your heart, making it weak, draining it of its desire to fight. When God allows terror to test us, it is for the purpose of perfecting our hearts. Imagine the fear Abraham must have felt as he drew back the knife to slay his beloved son Isaac. Yet it was that test that prepared Abraham to receive the blessing God had promised him when He first called him.

When Jesus petitioned His Father in the Garden of Gethsemane, the Bible says He was in agony. He was afraid of what lay ahead for Him. But the Greek word used here and translated "agony," is a word that means "a fear which trembles in the face of the issue, yet allows one to remain and face it."[1] Luke 22:44 says that Jesus, "being in an agony He prayed more earnestly." But if you look at the verse right before it, you'll see why He was able to pray more earnestly.

And there appeared an angel unto Him from heaven, strengthening Him (Luke 22:43).

Here is the key to making it through tests of terror. We have to seek help from God. Terror brings us to the limits of our faith, our knowledge, and our strength. And when we reach that point, there are only two things we can do: We can give in to the fear that threatens us, or we can give up and let God take over in us and for us. When I say "give up," I don't mean throw in the towel, of course. I mean surrender yourself to whatever God wants to do. Like Jesus, "nevertheless" your way to power from on high.

Browsing through one of my personal journals from 1992, I came upon a series of entries that so vividly recount a season where God allowed me to be tested to the limits of my faith, knowledge, and

---

1.   *The New International Hebrew/Greek Key Study Bible* (AMG International, Inc., 1984, 1991).

strength. Please allow me to share the contents of my heart in that season with you.

December 21, 1992: I was soon to leave on a three-day cruise to spend time with God as I tried to make sense of my husband's illness and its ramifications. I had called my friend and counselor Dr. Mary Simms, who had this to share:

God will take me on a journey to raise me to another level, another notch in Him. He will replace my neediness of Wayne with Himself. Now is the time for healing and wholeness—alone. God will become my strength. I will return whole.

December 23, 1992: *Today I make a quality, Godly decision to crucify the lusts of my flesh. I make a conscious, deliberate decision to put away wrath and evil thoughts or deeds. I decide for Christ. I decide with Christ. I decide in Christ.*

December 24, 1992: *It's not only Christmas Eve, but it's also the eve of a special time, place, and purpose in my life. I'm on the brink of a miracle. That which I cannot do myself, change, or edit, I can trust the almighty God to make the difference. I choose to love, I choose to commit, I choose the will of God, for He that hath begun a good work in me, shall perform it to the day of Christ. I trust God. I lean on God. I am in a spiritual labor room, awaiting, in pain, for the birth of something new, exciting, and supernatural. I won't faint. I won't give up. I shall not be moved, for I am like a tree planted by the water (Word) and I shall not be moved. God has not given me the spirit of fear, but of love, power, and a sound mind. I don't fear man. I fear God who made man. I may not know where my steps lead, but I know whose path I walk...Praise God!*

January 8, 1993: I was sitting in a medical trailer as technicians performed a CAT scan on my husband Wayne. They showed me on the film evidence that he had experienced a stroke and cranial bleeding.

God help me! I know You can. You're in charge, and I love You. I trust You...this too will pass! The Lord led me to Judges 6:12. *"The angel of the Lord appeared to him and said, 'Mighty soldier, the Lord is with you.'" Wanda, you are a good soldier, and I am with you. Fear not. What a wonderful reminder, throughout this challenge, God, that You have called me "Good Soldier." I am determined to be Your good soldier.*

January 11, 1993: Doctors believe that my husband has an inoperable brain tumor. Bishop T. Wesley Weeks, a friend of the family, came to visit Wayne in the hospital. He was gracious enough to minister to us at church. His sermon was titled "Why Me?" It was like water from a rock.

Bishop Weeks. Victory is my destiny. Success is my destiny. I am strongest at my weakest. Why me? For God's glory! He said every time you go through, God has something for you. Our place of power is reached by our experience of pain, for on the other side of pain is power! Allow yourself the pleasure of failure. God gives a test for a testimony.

January 12, 1993: The doctors have confirmed a "tumor mass." It's not infectious, so it's not treatable with drugs. It is inoperable because of its location. They are recommending radiation treatment in an attempt to shrink the tumor.

Your Good Thing Is on the Way. Psalm 34:1-3,8-10. Genesis 50:19-20. "I will bless the Lord at all times: His praise shall continually be in my mouth. My soul shall make her boast in the Lord: the humble shall hear thereof, and be glad. O magnify the Lord with me, and let us exalt His name together...O taste and see that the Lord is good: blessed is the man that trusteth in Him. O fear the Lord, ye His saints: for there is no want to them that fear Him. The young lions do lack, and suffer hunger: but they that seek the Lord shall not want any good thing." "Fear not: for am I in the place of God? But as for you, ye thought evil against me; but God meant it unto good, to bring to pass, as it is this day, to save much people alive."

January 13, 1993: *God, show me Your way, Your will, Your plan. They say Wayne has four to six months to live. God, that's just 120 to 180 days. Lord, what do **You** say? We believe You. We trust You. We love You, Jesus! Have Thine own way. I speak to pain, I speak to fear, I speak to white blood cells, I speak to an infiltrated right lung. I speak to infections that trigger fevers. I speak to neurons that cause memory loss, and I cure these symptoms and command that satan be bound and that healing arises. I send Your word, Jesus, to the bone marrow of Wayne and command it to flourish and be whole. Thank You, Lord, for stabilizing Wayne. I believe You, Lord, I trust You, Jesus. I do love You! You have promised me happiness, love, and blessings again and again!*

Weeks later, I watched my husband close his eyes and enter eternity. God had not allowed "my cup" to pass from me. As Wayne left this world to receive his healing on the other side, I was left alone among my "nevertheless." I had prayed all I could pray. I couldn't think of another doctor, another cure, another word of encouragement. I didn't have another smile with which to pretend or another "Thank you" for well-meaning friends. I had called out every Scripture I knew, rebuked every demon, and stood on every word of prophecy that would hold my weight. I had given over every burden, rejoiced, prayed without ceasing, pursued peace, run with patience, trusted, stood, cried out, and waited.

There was nothing left to do, think, pray, say, or be. I had nothing left. All I had was poured into the one who had just left me to be with the Lord. Then a new terror gripped me…How would I make it without him?

And there appeared an angel unto Him from heaven, strengthening Him (Luke 22:43).

He has said that He will never leave us nor forsake us (see Heb. 13:5). When I look back on that season, I know He did not lie. The Lord was there, even when I wasn't. He took care of me and my family. He took care of my church and every other obligation. He strengthened me in that season. He enlarged my heart in that season. Fear was not an option in that season. To choose it would have meant choosing death. And when I faced the terror of my life and chose Life, His perfect love cast out fear and planted new understanding, new patience, new wisdom, and new courage.

Complications that force change upon us are a fact of life. We waste our time in trying to avoid them or complain about them. Paul says we are to learn to be content no matter what's going on (see Phil. 4). That includes finding contentment in trouble, trial, and terror. But because each of them has a different purpose, our path to contentment in each of them is a different one.

Because the goal of trouble is obedience, our contentment in it is found only in our *fear* of God. The fear of the Lord is the beginning of wisdom, declares Proverbs again and again. Fear is described by Bishop Kenneth Ulmer in his book *Spiritually Fit to Run the Race* as a "two-sided coin." On one side is a holy reverence for God because of who He is. On the other side is a "holy afraid-ness" *of* God because of what He is capable of doing to us. It is the fear that a child should have of disobeying or disrespecting his parents, even though he looks up to them and knows they love him. Only a fool doesn't fear God. And we are foolish every time we choose to go our own way.

The goal of a trial is to prove you, so contentment in a trial is found only in *faith*. No matter how difficult your struggle is, a good, solid dose of faith is necessary for you to make it through the challenge and come out celebrating change. Faith has been defined as Forsaking All I Trust Him. And that's what we have to do. Like Job, we have to trust that God has His reasons for testing us. We have to believe that He will not leave us confounded or without hope. We have to know that all things, even the things that torture us at the moment, work together for our good, because we love Him and are called by Him (see Rom. 8:28).

Complications

Terror only leaves us two options: Give in or *focus*. When we face that crisis of soul and spirit, there is nothing within us that will get us through it. The only way to reach a place of terror is to reach your limit. It's like coming to the edge of a cliff and hearing God say, "Trust me and walk." At that point, you can't use your carnal eyes to see. You have to see with your spirit. You can't look back, because fear and its father the devil are in hot pursuit of you. And when they overtake you, they will destroy you. You can't look ahead, because what's before you is just as frightening. You have to focus all your attention on the One who promised to keep you.

Jonah, Job, and Jesus were given to us as gifts to help us obey, wait, and walk our way through complications to change. And we are given to others when we can stand as a testimony of God's faithfulness in testing us.

Change Your Mind

Our thoughts are not His thoughts. Our ways are not His ways. (See Isaiah 55:8.) It's hard to fathom sometimes how One who loves us so much allows such turmoil, fear, heartache, and destruction to enter our lives. But to question the love of God—who *is love*—is to question His very existence. "Do you love me?" is a question better left for your sweetheart on Valentine's Day. Do you believe that He is? Then seek Him diligently, and He will reward you with His love.

1. Go to the Book of Hebrews and review chapter 11, particularly the people mentioned in the "Hall of Faith." Choose three whose stories are recounted in detail in the Old Testament. Study them and list the troubles, trials, and/or terrors they encountered in their journey with God. How did the tests change them?

2. Are you a good "test taker"? How did you handle the most recent challenge in your Christian walk?

3. Can you think of three things in your life that you believe satan meant for evil, but God turned into good? Take a moment to thank Him again for loving you.

4. What could you tell someone that would help them avoid trouble you have encountered?

5. What could you tell someone that would help them wait on God through a trial?

6. Have you ever faced terror? How did you know you had come through it?

7. Read Deuteronomy 8 every day for one week. Pray and ask God to show you each day what it tells you about Him. Write it down. It will bless you for years to come.

"Once upon a time there was a man named Andrew Carnegie who lived in New Jersey with his two daughters Aneicka and Andrea..."

Change

Chapter Six

The Path of Most Resistance

Woe unto them that call evil good, and good evil; that put darkness for light, and light for darkness; that put bitter for sweet, and sweet for bitter!

—Isaiah 5:20

"Do you know that oftentimes a root has split a rock, when suffered to remain in it? Give no lodgement to the seed of evil, seeing that it will break up your faith."

—St. Cyril of Jerusalem

"The good life exists only when we stop wanting a better one. The itch for things is a virus draining the soul of contentment."

—Unknown

"All that is necessary for the triumph of evil is for good men to do nothing."

—Edmund Burke

Suppose you chose not to celebrate change. What are your alternatives? Well, you have three: 1) You can choose something other than change. 2) You can choose something other than celebration. 3) You can choose not to choose. The first choice is *sin*. The second choice is *discontentment*. The third choice is *complacency*. These three are the enemies of God-ordained change and celebration.

Like all things that rebel against God, these things seek to pull us away from our destiny and deny us the prize we were put on this earth to receive. I'm not talking about a job, or money, or a husband, or anything else so temporal. I'm talking about eternal life. You see, while you're fighting with God about changing, the devil is battling it out in the heavenlies for your soul. He doesn't care about your rejecting change *per se*. But he knows that anything you reject from God takes you further from Him.

Do you know how sheep get lost? They graze with their heads down. They don't pay attention to anything but their own hunger and satisfying it. If they nibble away from the rest of the flock, they become tasty prey for a ravenous wolf—a wolf who's been waiting for just such a moment. Giving in to sin, discontentment, or complacency, no matter how small a thing you think it is, will take you away from the safety of the Shepherd's care.

Sin

You knew we'd come to this. You can't deal with anything God wants you to do without culling out anything that might prevent you from doing it. Celebrating change is impossible in an atmosphere of sin. A sinful mind resists godly change. A sinful heart rejects godly celebration. And sinful behavior always follows the heart and mind.

I'm not going to take you on a long, convoluted, time-consuming journey into the nature and origin of sin. That's another book for another time. (Actually, it's quite a few books.) For our purposes here, we'll define sin *as any behavior or belief that falls short in any way of loving God with your whole mind, heart, soul and might, or falls short of loving your neighbor as yourself.* Now that I've managed to catch us all up in the same net and put us in the same boat (for all have sinned), let's get real.

I speak to you from the bottom of my heart, with the boldness of Jeremiah, unafraid of your faces. Before we can be free to celebrate change, we have to be set free by the Truth. Notice I did not say we have to be set free by things that are *true*. Jesus is the Truth. God set Him before us as the standard, and we have the power to live up to that standard. But too many of us are choosing to live a lie. So much of what we do is for the purpose of creating an image in the eyes of men, to win their approval or accolades. We sing louder than anybody around us at church, then go home and cuss folks just as loud. We don't even consider that God is with us Monday through Saturday too, and that He is not pleased.

The reason we tolerate sin in our lives is that we have stopped using Jesus as our standard and set ourselves up as the standard for the world we live in. How many times have you looked at what your neighbor is doing and thought, *I'm not sinning like that*. In that moment, you felt like you were a little closer to God than they were, didn't you?

Or do you find yourself "classifying" your sin? Fornication isn't as bad if you've only got one partner, if you plan to marry, or if you both go to church. Murder is worse than lying, and of course "white lies" aren't as bad as "bold-faced" ones. Gossip that is true is just conversation, really. It's okay to stop speaking to someone because they didn't repay a loan, because the wicked borrow and don't pay it back, and I can mistreat you if I condemn you as wicked first. And it's okay to ignore a homeless man begging for money if I think he looks able enough to work for a living.

But we love the Lord, don't we? We are fearfully and wonderfully made, aren't we? We can do all things through Christ, can't we? We are called, set aside, appointed, anointed, blood-bought, water-washed, precious little lambs, King's kids, born-again, holy hand-laying, demon-slaying, harp-playing, in the Spirit praying, supplicating, patiently waiting, devil-hating, resurrection power-possessing prophets and prophetesses, on our way to Heaven anyhow! Ready to go right now, right? Wrong!

Sin is sin, and if you're in it, you can't win it! God has never had a problem with sinners acting like sinners, or saints acting like saints. His nostrils flare when saints act like sinners, which, if you think about it, amounts to the same thing as a sinner acting like a saint. Don't be deceived. God is not mocked. We reap what we sow. (See Galatians 6:7.) When you come into His holy sanctuary and lift dirty, filthy hands in hypocritical worship, you're not fooling God. Man may think you're deep in worship and even believe your performance, but God does not accept such empty gestures.

Do I seem harsh? Well, God takes sin very seriously, because His love for you is very serious business to Him. He has plotted out every moment of your life (see Ps. 139:16), planned every good work (Eph. 2:10), defeated every attack of the enemy (Is. 54:17), and has blessed you with everything you need to live right (2 Pet. 1:3). And every time you choose not to go where He directs you, or in other words, every time you sin, you move yourself a little further away from what He wants to do with you, in you, for you, to you, and through you. So when He asks us to change, or embrace change, and we choose another path, we have moved out of the range of His promises to us.

Sin keeps us from the blessing of celebrating change in three ways. First, it dulls our senses and makes it harder for us to hear and therefore respond to God-directed changes. When we go in a direction away from God through sin, we have separated ourselves from the True Vine. Jesus tells us in John 15 that every branch that is not in Him is cast into the fire. I know you're saying, "I'm saved. I'm 'in Him.'" But are you bearing fruit? If you're in sin, you're not bearing fruit. And He says that every branch in Him that isn't bearing fruit, He'll take away. Now if you're bearing some fruit, He'll prune you—or cut away those areas that aren't contributing to your fruit-production potential—so that you'll bear more.

Imagine you're in a conversation with someone and, as they're talking, you walk into another room. The further away you get, the harder it becomes to hear what they are saying. You'll either have to ask them to speak louder or you'll have to go back to the room where they are to hear them. Now if you keep asking them to talk louder and never return from the other room, they might get the impression—the correct impression—that you aren't as concerned about what they're saying as you seemed to be at the beginning of the conversation. And they'll probably stop talking until you decide to return to them.

Does that sound familiar at all? We dibble and dabble in sin while we pretend to be interested in the things of God. We say we love Him and want to be in His presence, but while He's trying to talk to us, we're off "in another place." Eventually, He stops talking and waits for you to come back.

And while you're in your sin and God is not speaking to you, you are without the power of His Holy Spirit. You may not notice it at first, but after a while you'll see that your prayers go up about as far as the ceiling and return to you void. Your praise starts to sound like clanging brass. Your gifts become corrupted. This weakness is the second way sin keeps us from celebrating change.

Have you seen what happens to a garden that hasn't been watered? The ground eventually dries up, and even water poured onto it just rolls away and isn't absorbed. When our hearts become "dry" and "parched" because of our sin, even the water of the Word won't penetrate it. But in nature, the air continues to put pressure on dry ground through evaporation until every drop of moisture, seen and unseen, is sucked up. Then the pressure eventually causes the ground to crack and splinter. David said in Psalm 32:3-4 that when he sinned and kept silent about it, his moisture, symbolic of his spiritual health, was turned into a drought.

When drought occurs, the only thing that will save the cracked, stony ground is heavy, continuous rain that forces moisture back into it. In Psalm 32:5 David says he confessed his sin, and God forgave him. Then in verse 6 he exhorts us to trust God and pray to Him while He may be found so that "surely in the floods of great waters they shall not come nigh...."

Wait a minute. We had a drought in verse 4, and now we have a flood two verses later? The way the text lays out, the flood was inevitable. But because David confessed his sin and was forgiven, the flood didn't destroy him. In fact, in 32:7 he says he made God his hiding place to "preserve me from trouble." Ah, there's our friend "trouble" from the previous chapter—a complication introduced into our lives to force a change from disobedience to obedience. God is merciful, isn't He?

Finally, sin keeps us from celebrating change by blurring the path we're on. There's an old proverb that says, "If you don't know where you're going, any road will get you there." Sin is like that. The road is wide and there are a lot of folks on it, but it leads to so many different places before it eventually gets to death.

When you obey God, there is one road to follow. It may be narrow and steep at times, but it is straight and leads to only one place. And each act of obedience keeps you on that road, including obedience regarding change. If God has ordained a change for you, and you comply, then you stay on the road. Now when you get off the path, suddenly there will appear before you a hundred different ways to go. At first this seems like more freedom. But eventually you'll find yourself trapped and confused, and like all lost sheep, crying out for help. The problem is that, depending on the road you took, the wolves might reach you before the Shepherd does. Are you willing to take that chance?

The remedy for sin is simple. It's not always easy, but it is simple. *Walk in the light.* John says God is light (see 1 Jn. 1:5). All things are clear when we walk in the light. Our senses aren't dull when we walk with God. The source of our strength lives in us when we walk in the light, so that we don't have to give in to sin. The path is visible when we walk in the light. There may be obstacles, pits, and serpents on it, but at least we can see them. When we choose to walk in the light of our heavenly Father and not in the darkness of sin, we welcome change because we see the hand of God. When we walk in the light, we are able to see and therefore acknowledge in all our ways the One who directs our path.

Discontentment

Why is it so important to *celebrate* change? Why can't we just endure, tolerate, accept, adapt, or adopt it without celebrating it? Let me ask you this. If you mailed a gift to someone, how would you know if they received it? How would you know they liked it? How would you feel if they didn't even acknowledge that they had gotten it or that they knew you had sent it? What if you went by their house and saw it still in the box, or worse, in the garbage can waiting for pickup? Would you give them that same gift next year if you thought they didn't like it? And what if you ran into them and they told you they didn't even know you had sent them the gift because they hadn't bothered to read the card?

Every good thing comes from God (see Jas. 1:17). It follows then that everything God gives is good and deserves to be acknowledged and appreciated. David said he would "bless the Lord at all times" (Ps. 34:1), not just when things went the way he thought they ought to go. And if the truth were told, things *always* do go our way. Romans 8:28 tells us that all things work together for our good. Then Paul tells us in Philippians 4:4 to rejoice in the Lord always. And I should note here that Paul wrote the Book of Philippians from a prison cell where he was being persecuted and threatened with death and his religion was being mocked and scorned by fellow prisoners. Still, he said to rejoice, not once in that verse, but twice!

Discontentment—the refusal to celebrate change—can be detrimental to our relationship with God. You see, the celebration is not for God, it's for us. God is not going to be less God because we refuse to praise Him or thank Him for His blessings. But thanksgiving gets us through His gates and praise gets us into His courts. Celebration ushers us into God's presence where we can worship Him and be further changed when we behold His glory (see 2 Cor. 3:18). Discontentment will keep us "outside" and away from the loving-kindness of our Lord, who just wants us to be close to Him so He can bless us all the more.

In addition to distancing us from God, discontentment also weakens our faith and the faith of those who know us. When we are discontent, we are not giving God proper credit for His activity in our lives. When we don't celebrate His gifts of change, we steal His glory. When others look at our lives, they do not see the joy of the Lord. They see someone who acts like God has forsaken them. In other words, they see a lie. And when we hold back the truth from them, we are holding back life from them. Jesus did say He is the Way, the Truth, and *the Life* (see Jn. 14:6). When you don't show people Jesus, you're showing them something that is not life-giving, life-affirming, or life-producing.

Do you realize that every time you tell someone a lie about Jesus, you are offering that person a tiny slice of death? Think about it. Sometimes the closest people get to Jesus is to the Jesus they see in you. And if you're showing them that a life with Jesus is something to hang your head about, it's no wonder they won't go to church! Would you be encouraged to follow a God who constantly disappointed someone you love?

A discontented heart will lie to you as well. If you believe that a change God has orchestrated in your life was not for your good, how likely are you going to be to seek God's counsel in the future? Until and unless we embrace and get excited about whatever changes God allows in our lives, we put ourselves in danger of avoiding His direction the next time we are faced with changing.

The remedy for discontentment is knowledge. Whenever we are unsatisfied with our lives, it is a sure sign that we are lacking in our understanding of God. To know Him is to know His ways and His Word, and by that, His will. To know Him is to know who we are in Him and how much He loves us. Content people don't question God's love, no matter what their circumstances are.

The biggest problem with discontentment when it comes to change is that it opens the door to so many other things like covetousness, jealousy, greed, anger, bitterness, and lust. If these things are allowed to take root in our hearts, then when they spring forth, they will have already corrupted us from the inside out. Discontentment makes it impossible to run our race with patience because it heaps upon our spirits the sin of murmuring, complaining, and unbelief. Beware lest you fall after the same pattern of the children of Israel who were not permitted to enter God's everlasting rest. Rest and discontentment cannot co-exist.

Complacency

Complacency is an arrogant sin. It is arrogant because it publicly chooses not to acquiesce to God's request for change. It is sin because it is dishonest and deceitful. It parades as everything but what it is. On the surface, complacent people look content. They appear confident. To the untrained spiritual eye, they portray faith. In truth, that contentment is apathy, the confidence is pride, and the faith is in fact fear.

Complacency is defined as "a feeling of quiet pleasure or security often while unaware or unconcerned with unpleasant realities."[1] It is self-satisfaction. In our context, complacency is the act of avoiding change for one of three reasons: 1) We don't know what lies ahead and we are afraid. 2) We know what's ahead and we don't like it. 3) We don't care what's ahead. We'd rather plot our own course.

When we avoid change because of our fear, we have made God to be a liar. When we complicate matters by pretending to be satisfied where we are, we have made ourselves to be liars. God did not give us a spirit of fear, but we do find ourselves in possession of it often. In Scripture, "Fear not" is usually the first thing God has to tell His people before they have to deal with change. Try doing a Bible study of every instance where God told His people, either directly or through prophets, not to be afraid. I promise that it can keep you busy for years.

God is not concerned that we have fear. He expects that. But He is concerned with how we handle it. Complacency is often a ploy to keep us from facing the fear of change, which is, in reality, giving in to fear, which is abandoning our faith. And that is of great concern to God.

So how do we handle the fear that comes with the prospect of change? First and foremost, we face it with the truth. Not facts, but truth. The facts may tell you that moving out of your boyfriend's house will be impossible because you can't make rent by yourself. But the truth is that your God shall (not might) supply all your needs according to His riches (not yours) (see Phil. 4:19).

The facts may tell you that you can't make it without those drugs, but the truth is you are more than a conqueror (see Rom. 8:37). The facts

---

1. *Merriam-Webster's Collegiate Dictionary*, Tenth ed. (Springfield, MA: Merriam-Webster, Inc., 1993), **complacency**.

may tell you that you are 40 years old and no one is going to want to marry you. But the truth is if you delight yourself in the Lord and trust Him, He will give you the desires of your heart (see Ps. 37:4). The truth is if you abide in Christ and His Word abides in you, you shall ask and it will be done (see Jn. 15:7). The facts may tell you that your parents can't afford to send you to college, but the truth is God gives us the power to get wealth (see Deut. 8:18).

We can't deal with fear by lying about it. We may as well deal with lung cancer by smoking a pack of cigarettes a day! That sounds ridiculous to you, doesn't it? But if God did not give you a spirit of fear, who do you think gave it to you? So you deal with something you got from the father of lies by lying? Come on, now.

Brother, you know in your heart that God has shown you your wife. But you're so afraid of losing your "Mack status," you're not going to move forward with her. Instead, you tell her, "things are good the way they are, baby," or "If it ain't broke, don't fix it." But let me tell you right here, man of God, if you don't embrace this change, you may not be able to embrace your destiny, and God will find her another Adam to complete.

Sister, you can keep that weight on if you want to. And you can tell all your friends that you are a "big, beautiful, proud woman of God." And you can cry yourself to sleep at night, because you don't want to be that big, but you don't believe you can change. But God has told you to be a good steward over that body He has gifted you with. He has told you to change your eating habits and stop making food your idol and your weight a dubious badge of honor. And He never tells you to do anything He hasn't already given you the power to do. So don't hide your fear. Tell Him about it. Then give it to Him. But don't hold onto it.

Fear is like junk mail. We get it. We don't want it. We really don't have any use for it. And we don't have to keep it. We can toss it out with all the other garbage satan sends our way. Faith, my friend, is the "fear-buster" we have in our arsenal of spiritual weapons. Ephesians 6:16 says, "Above all, [take] the shield of faith, wherewith ye shall be able to quench all the fiery darts of the wicked." "Above all," it says. That means if you don't take anything else to fight with, take your faith. Faith will extinguish every flaming arrow the enemy throws at you, including fear.

Complacency also can serve as a cover for knowing what's ahead and not liking it. This is pride. We tell God that we don't think He's doing a very good job with us. We refuse to change because we reject the change. But we don't want to tell others that. We wouldn't "look holy" if we told the truth, which is we just don't like what God is proposing. There are pastors, caught up in sin, who are scattering their flock and destroying relationships among their peers. God has told them to step down. "Let somebody else shepherd this people until you get your life together." But they continue where they are, refusing to change while people are dying in their care.

This kind of complacency—the refusal to honor the change or the God who called for it—is dangerous. God says He resists the proud (see Jas 4:6). That means He deliberately sets Himself against the proud. It is the picture of two football players on opposite teams facing each other at the line of scrimmage. You're set, waiting for the snap. And God says that if you think you're big and bad enough to take Him on, come on with it! He will mow you down at the appropriate time. Don't fool yourself into thinking that He will give you a merciful tap, either. The fact that He will flatten you is His greatest act of mercy toward you. Because if He lets you remain standing, somebody else might look at you and think it's okay to get up in God's face and try to take Him out.

First Peter 5:5 tells us to be "clothed with humility: for God resisteth the proud, and giveth grace to the humble." Which would you rather have? When God offers you change that's hard to swallow, take a deep breath and swallow it. If you don't, your choice to resist will come back to swallow you. Peter says that God gives grace to the humble. The humble are those who understand that He is the God who sits high and looks low. To them, He is gracious. To that one who is willing to embrace change and defer to the intelligence, wisdom, and foresight of an omniscient God, grace is given. And God's grace is sufficient in all things. Peter goes on to say in the next verse that if you humble yourself under God's mighty hand, He will exalt you "in due time."

So here are your choices when it comes to making changes you don't like. Change now, receive grace, and be exalted later. Or, don't change now and get clobbered; then receive the grace of being made low. Pick one.

Finally, we choose complacency over change because we are genuinely satisfied with our lives the way they are. It's a subtle difference between this type of complacency and the last. With the former, we reject change because we don't like the change. Here, we ignore the charge to change because we don't want to abandon what we already have. We don't really care what God is offering; we're not buying. We are satisfied, even comfortable, with the status quo.

There are two problems with apathy. First, as with pride, we presume to put ourselves on the level of decision-maker with God. The second and more ominous issue is that God has ceased to be the center and focus of our lives. The truth is that all sin is an act of choosing yourself over God. But apathy has the nerve to tell Him so to His face.

I've known people who have enjoyed a good level of professional and financial success whom God has called to a deeper commitment in their walk with Him. They give liberally of their talent and resources. But God is asking them to change some things in their lives and give Him their hearts. Wake up early and commune with Him. Forego some of those vacations to Vail in the winter and Europe in the summer and spend more time in the Word. Quit all that casual dating and commit to one virtuous woman or godly man. But life is too good the way it is.

Is that you? You hear God calling you to change. You know it's Him. But life is too good the way it is. You'd rather sleep in than pray. You'd rather ski, travel, or play than study the Word. That girlfriend or boyfriend is fit, fine, and financially stable, and they're not trying to "tie you down." And all you see is God swinging that ball and chain in your face. "I hear You, Lord. And I love You…but not *that* much."

When we are complacent due to apathy, we send God an engraved invitation to shake us up. And because we're so satisfied with our lives, we usually don't see it coming. The invitation went out without our knowing it, but God will show up, and He will cause a whole lot of shaking. How many times have you seen people, with seemingly perfect lives, suddenly devastated by some great calamity? A perfectly healthy young man struck down by a heart attack; a car wreck cripples someone else. One day all is well. The next day, all is changed.

Sometimes tragedy strikes not because we are self-satisfied or apathetic about change, but because God has in His sovereignty chosen to prove your faith. That is not what I'm talking about here. I want you to know here that there is a very real danger in apathy of inviting a wilderness experience, or worse, of inviting God to ignore *you* until you choose to bring your prodigal behind home.

Are you in an apathetic state of complacency? Sometimes it's hard to tell, especially if you have been living that way for a long time. But there are some indicators. Do any or all of these apply to you?

Quiet versus peaceful. When there is a "lack of noise" in our lives, we can sometimes mistake that for peace. But peace is not something that eliminates every sound. Peace is that environment of the spirit that makes God easier to hear. Are you hearing God? "Faith cometh by hearing, and hearing by the word of God" (Rom. 10:17). If nothing is being said in your spirit, if the Word that is supposed to abide in you is not making itself known within you, you may be in need of a little more one-on-one time with God.

Happiness versus joy. Do you have joy, or is happiness the yardstick by which you measure your relationship with God? Happiness has to do with "happenings." Happiness is the result of being pleased with how your situation, circumstances, and environment make you feel. When they change, so does your level of happiness. Joy, on the other hand, is that state of being satisfied and pleased with something that is unchangeable; that is, God. We are precious and bought with a price; that gives us joy. And it is true no matter what our circumstances are.

The joy of the Lord is our strength (see Neh. 8:10). That means the tougher things get to handle, the more joy we have access to. Our "happiness" with the Lord might be worth a shout or two when we get a promotion or buy a new house. But our joy in the Lord will mean the difference between life and death when Satan attacks. Complacent people are happy people. Contented people have joy.

Seeking control versus seeking order. Complacent people seek to control their environment so that it continues to serve them the way they want it to. When we abandon the safety of complacency for the contentment that can come only by faith, we give up seeking control and seek order instead.

Control must be seized. Order is followed. Control is dependent on my personal ability to hold on to it. Order never changes, so I only have to be "strong" enough to see it. Control means I have to determine my destination and my path. Order has already established where I'm going and the best path to getting there. Control is about me; order is about God. Control is established when my strength is established. Order was established before the world was framed. Control can be taken away from me, while order is God-given. It can't be taken away. The end has already been called from the beginning by the One who is Himself the beginning and the end. We'll talk more about order in the next chapter.

Complacency resists change. To one who is content, change is welcome and celebration is mandatory. Complacency rests assured in self. But when we do things God's way, we learn early on that we cannot be counted on for much of anything. It's no accident that Jesus calls us sheep. Sheep have no natural defense mechanisms. All they really know how to do well is get lost, cry for help, distinguish their shepherd's voice, and follow whoever is leading them (and they really don't care who's leading them until they develop a relationship with their shepherd, which takes time).

The only cure for complacency is to press. Pressing into God, inclining your ear, and setting your affections on Him, is the only way to get to what your soul really needs, and that is the Truth. But this is truth gotten at a price. When you press, you make a quality decision to reestablish God as the center of your life. Apathetic complacency deems God not important enough to warrant our attention.

When we press, we recommit ourselves to true, Spirit-infused worship. And that can't occur unless God becomes the sum and substance of all that you do. He must be the object and the source of all your desires. You determine to seek Him first and allow Him to add to your life such as He would impart unto you. You abandon your old behavior of waiting for things to give you permission to praise Him. You create a life out of your time spent with Him; you do not create time to spend with Him out of your life.

Every hindrance to celebrating change is satan's attempt to give you possession, position, or power without God. His goal is to rob you of your destiny, which is to be loved and cherished by the One who made you for just that purpose. Tell satan no. Tell him you've tried it his way and now you're going to try *the* Way. Know, child of God, that you can have victory, if you want it. The question is, how badly do you want it?

John 5:2-9 tells the story of a man who waited at the pool of Bethesda to be healed from an infirmity. He had been going to the pools for 38 years, but there was no one there who would put him into the healing water when the right time came. Scripture says Jesus saw him and knew that he had been sick for a long time and asked him, "Wilt thou be made whole?" In other words, "Do you want to be healed?"

That seems like such an obvious question, when you think about it. The man is sick. He waits by the healing pools. Obviously he wants to be healed, or he wouldn't be there. We go to church Sunday in and Sunday out. The church is a place where we're supposed to get healed. And we've got sin in our lives. Obviously we want to be free of our sin, or we wouldn't be there, right? Right?

We don't have to be slaves to sin, discontentment, and complacency. We have the power of the Holy Spirit, which is the Spirit of Truth. We have in us the same power that raised Jesus from the dead. Our faith can move mountains and quench the arrows of wickedness. And yet we still struggle with celebrating change. We struggle with peace, joy, and contentment. We struggle with conceiving, believing, and receiving the love of God. We're weak and impotent. We do all the things that make it look like we want to be holy, fired-up saints. Then Jesus, the Truth, walks up and asks us, "Do you want to be made whole?" Well, do you?

Change Your Mind

Man looks at the outward appearance, but God looks at the heart. How does your heart look? How loud is the praise party that's going on in your mind? What color is your worship in a dark prayer closet? How deep, wide, and fast-flowing is that river of joy that no one can see but you?

A lot of people say they know God. But a lot of folks know God like they know the President. They know where He lives, but they don't really hang out with Him. They know people who know Him, but not many of them have had dinner with Him, either. But unlike the President, you don't have to be important to the world for Him to invite you over. What's stopping you? And by the way, when you see Him, tell Him Wanda says hello. He'll know who you're talking about. We go way back.

1.   What is the "smallest" sin you indulge in your life?

2.   What is the "biggest" sin you struggle with?

3.   On a scale of 1 to 10, how "good" are you?

4.   Most of us have answers to questions 1 through 3 even if we don't write them down. Take a moment to consider why we classify and compare ourselves when it comes to sin and righteousness. How did you feel about yourself after answering those questions?

5.   List three areas of your life where you are not satisfied. Now determine whether you are complacent or content in those areas.

6.   Write God a letter of gratitude for the three areas you listed in question #5. If they were issues in someone else's life, how would you encourage that person?

"Once upon a time there was a man named Andrew Carnegie who lived in New Jersey with his two daughters Aneicka and Andrea, and he traveled to California..."

Change

Chapter Seven

Hidden Treasure

He hath made every thing beautiful in his time: also He hath set the world in their heart, so that no man can find out the work that God maketh from the beginning to the end.

—Ecclesiastes 3:11

"Go Godward: thou wilt find a road."

—Russian proverb

"Disown the idea of an abiding God as the Creator and the ultimate end of all men, and you can only have peoples in various times and places, each working for its own ends in terms of their own time and place. Hence place must forever war against place, and time against time."

—Louis J.A. Mercier

So you think you've got a handle on change? Are you clear on celebration, certain that you can handle anything that comes your way? Then let's look at the bigger picture, and, I promise, you'll never look at celebrating change the same way again.

I'd like to shift your perspective a bit. Same pool, deeper water. This may seem odd so far into the book, but I want you to see and understand God's pattern of relationship with us. We don't learn everything there is to know about God at the moment of our salvation. We learn just enough to get us to the next point of revelation, which prepares us for the next one, and so on.

This process of "progressive revelation" walks in tandem with God's tendency toward "progressive specificity," and together these two work, over time, to increase our capacity to ingest, digest, and reflect Him. Now that's my $10 way of saying the more you know God, the more He shows you of Himself, and the more He shows you of Himself, the more He shows you in Himself. And the more you see of Him and in Him, the better you become at receiving and reflecting His divine nature. Paul says as much in Second Corinthians 3:18:

> *But we all, with open face beholding as in a glass the glory of the Lord, are changed into the same image from glory to glory, even as by the Spirit of the Lord.*

Look at the same verse in the New Living Translation:

> *And all of us have had that veil removed so that we can be mirrors that brightly reflect the glory of the Lord, And as the Spirit of the Lord works within us, we become more and more like Him and reflect His glory even more.*

Why is this so important, and why now? *I'm already dancing because I already know what I'm going to say.* I want you to see the glorious purpose for celebrating change. We could stop at embracing it for bringing us unexpected blessings and success. We could be satisfied to know that change strengthens us and proves our faith. We could accept with gratitude that submitting to change keeps us from sin, gives us access to joy, and cultivates peace within us, and call it a day. But to stop there would be to truncate the blessing God intended for you in these pages.

Change is so much more than "here today, different tomorrow." It's not just a night's weeping endured until morning. It goes way past the renewing of our minds and spiritual fruit-bearing. *Change is God's way of preparing us for what He has prepared for us.* And that is so much more than what we can see, taste, think, buy, give, wish for, speak, or even have faith for. And it never, ever ends. We serve an infinite God, who was long before every yesterday and will be long after the last to-morrow lives. And our very lives are in Him! Change is not just about what goes on in my life, our lives, or on this earth. Change is a never-ending journey into the heart of God!

Take your mind off of the mundane things of this earth. Let it travel, unfettered, past the end of time itself to a place where there is no day, no night, no time, no sorrow, no care, no sickness, and no fear or dread. A place where no hands have toiled, but there is no lack. A place where life everlasting, joy unspeakable, perfect peace, perpetual praise, and worship in spirit and truth are the only items on your list of things to do, every day, forever and ever. And every moment only makes it more so. My Lord! Change brings us to exceeding abundance and beyond to where no eye has seen, nor ear heard, nor heart imagined. This is the promise of change. And change is the very reason we pray to God.

Look at the response of Jesus in Matthew 6:9-13 to the disciples' desire to know how to pray (the disciples' asking is recounted in Luke 11:1):

After this manner therefore pray ye: Our Father which art in heaven, Hallowed be Thy name. Thy kingdom come. Thy will be done in earth, as it is in heaven. Give us this day our daily bread. And forgive us our debts, as we forgive our debtors. And lead us not into temptation, but deliver us from evil: for Thine is the kingdom, and the power, and the glory, for ever. Amen.

"Thy kingdom come." In other words, let Your reign and rule come to include us. "Thy will be done in earth, as it is in heaven." This is a more specific rendering of the preceding sentence. Lord, we want You to reign here over us. That means we want You to have Your way here on earth, the way You already do in Heaven. *Change things here, so they'll be more like they already are where we're going.*

125

Then Jesus outlines the process by which the change will take place. "Give us this day our daily bread." You feed someone so they can live and grow (*change*). "And forgive us our debts, as we forgive our debtors." This means forgive us our offenses *in the same manner* that we forgive those who have offended us. Now we know that we can be low-down when we want to with people. But this prayer says we are willing to be treated the way we treat others. Obviously this prayer implies that we plan to be more Godly in our responses to people (*change*).

"And lead us not into temptation, but deliver us from evil." We don't want God to lead us to sin, but we want Him to deliver us from wickedness. That seems like a contradiction. Don't lead me to sin, but deliver me from it. The truth is God doesn't lead us to sin, but we will certainly find a way to do it on our own, won't we? Then He has to deliver us from it. That word *deliver* means to draw out with force or violence. One of two things is happening here. Either we're not trying to get out of our sin and God has to drag us out, or satan has such a hold on us that we are powerless against him and God has to drag us out. This part of the prayer is asking God to find us in our dangerous sinful circumstances and save us (*change* our situation).

"For Thine is the kingdom, and the power, and the glory, for ever. Amen." This last statement declares everything else in the prayer to be done. We asked that His Kingdom would come. Here we say the Kingdom belongs to Him. We then declare that all power to make that happen belongs to Him, and that all the glory for making it happen belongs to Him too. *Change* the earth, Lord. We know You have the power to do it, and we'll give You all the glory now and forever for what You're going to do.

This prayer that we call "The Lord's Prayer," is really a prayer for us. It's a prayer for change, and it is one that He has been answering since before the world was made. Our struggles with change seem so small and unnecessary when seen through the lens of this holy petition. Every prayer we pray should fit this pattern given to us by Jesus. Every prayer should seek to get us closer to God's Kingdom coming on this earth. So every prayer we pray is in fact a prayer for change. And every change, therefore, has an aim, a direction, and an end.

Divine Order

Now that you understand how change works for you, in you, and through you, you should understand that change in your individual life is a very, very small part of a very large, complex, glorious plan designed and orchestrated by God. When we face changes in our lives, they appear monumental to us. And it's so easy to get caught up in and consumed by how much of our effort, emotions, and ego go into dealing with the sifting and shaking that goes on in our little consciousness, let alone how other people's changes affect us.

But imagine this: Each one of the million changes that happen to you in your lifetime, multiplied by the millions of changes that happen to each of the billions of other people on the earth, multiplied by the trillions of changes that happen *in* and *to* the earth, multiplied by the infinite sextillions (1 followed by 21 zeros) of changes that happen throughout the universe—is being tracked and tallied by an all-knowing, all-seeing, ever-present God whose plans and thoughts extend beyond all those changes. (And yet, He still has time to make sure the pecan praline ice cream is on the shelf at the supermarket on the very day that you happen to really crave it.) It is this most incredible Being whose love is as unfathomable as our need for it is unquenchable, who established change—all change—to serve His order.

I'm trying to get you to see change not as something that just happens to you, or to others, or even just on earth. I want you to see that it is a part of a divine progression that we neither conceived nor control. Change is planned and positioned to move us along in life according to God's established order. When Paul exhorts us to "walk in the Spirit," he is telling us simply to walk according to God's order (see Gal. 5). Why? He tells us in Ephesians 1:4-11 that God chose us before He made the world to be His holy children, not because we were so special, but because it pleased Him.

So, knowing that we were nowhere near holy, He sacrificed His Son to save us. He accepted us as beloved, forgave us, and took on the responsibility of changing us so that we would one day be able, in the fullness of time, to be with Him in Heaven and receive the inheritance He has already set aside for us. Why? Ephesians 1:11 says because He felt like it!

I praise God for His grace. Change seems like so much trouble to me sometimes, until I realize that all the effort is really God's. We live such self-centered lives, thinking until we can't think anymore about how this or that change will make us look, feel, or act. Where will I go if I move from this place? What will I do if I turn from that thing? Who will leave me if I speak this word or give up this job? If I change the way I dress, how many men will stop looking at me? If I give up that car, that watch, or those friends, what will become of me?

But God, God, *God in Heaven* is working to make it possible for us to live with Him forever just so He can love us. Us! Not perfect, holy, angelic, blameless, spirits—us! And we struggle. We strive against Him who could extinguish the universe with one blast from His nostrils. We complain about doing the will of One who took off His glory to come down to this filthy mound of earth to be ridiculed and spat upon, *by us*, for what He saw as the privilege of loving us. Us! How small a price is change to pay to the One who not only wants to give us eternity, but Himself in the bargain? Us!

The Components of Order

Purpose, *time*, and *season* are the three components of order. They work independently and in combination to maintain God's order in our lives. Purpose is defined here as the sum of the goals, reasons, and/or activities for which you were placed on this earth. Birth is the beginning of a lifelong journey to fully realize every purpose God ordained for you. We do not accomplish every one. If we did, our lives would have been lived to perfection, and only Jesus is perfect. But there are some purposes that are "non-negotiable," meaning there are some purposes that God will not let us out of for any reason. And He will navigate our steps, sometimes by force, to see that they're accomplished.

John the Baptist was anointed in his mother's womb for his purpose, to herald and baptize the Son of God. It was not an accident that John was beheaded just before Jesus began His public ministry. John himself said with great joy, "He must increase, but I must decrease" (Jn. 3:30). He knew his purpose on earth was fulfilled.

Time is that collection of moments that comprise our existence on earth from the time we are born until the time we die. Our time on earth is fixed. David asked God to reveal to him the measure of his days so he'd understand just how short his life really was. Because God knows why He put us all here; He knows exactly how long each of us needs to accomplish everything He ordained for us to accomplish.

The concept of season is threefold. First, it is that specific point in time wherein a particular event is ordained to occur. That is a thing's "full season." Secondly, it is a span of moments that make up a period of time where a specific event or series of events is *supposed* to occur. For example, the children of Israel were given a season following their deliverance from Egypt to learn to trust God. When that time expired, the Lord's wrath was kindled and all but Caleb and Joshua were condemned to die in the wilderness and never see the Promised Land. Finally, a season refers to that recurring span of time marked by particular characteristics unique to it. There are, for instance, seasons for planting, harvesting, living, dying, and so on. The "winters" of our lives are marked by little or no production and the need to trust God's provision, whereas "spring" is a time of rebirth.

Purpose, time, and season work together to serve God's order. They are subject to the will of God, and when we choose to live according to the will of God, we become subject to them. With that in mind, we see change in a different light. Change is:

Purpose, time, and season, acting upon us, around us, and between us, to serve God's established order, to fulfill His ultimate goal to love us fully and be fully loved by us forever.

It seems almost ludicrous now to focus our attention on the effects of change. It seems an unavoidable fact of our existence. But Scripture says God's ways are not our ways and that His thoughts are not ours (see Is. 55:8). How do we know then what choices to make and when to make them? How do we understand the order of God so that we know which changes are ordained by Him? Remember that living according to God's order is walking by the Spirit. God has given every Christian His Spirit. And that Spirit is there to discern the things of God for us. First Corinthians 2:9-10,12 says:

> *But as it is written, Eye hath not seen, nor ear heard, neither have entered into the heart of man, the things which God hath prepared for them that love Him. But God hath revealed them unto us by His Spirit: for the Spirit searcheth all things, yea, the deep things of God....Now we have received, not the spirit of the world, but the spirit which is of God; that we might know the things that are freely given to us of God.*

When we walk in the Spirit, we are given spiritual eyes to see the things that God is doing in our lives.

When we see change in the context of God's order, it's not only easier to accept, it's also easier to celebrate, because we know whose hand we're in. But some of us are too busy fussing and fighting about having to make changes to see what's going on. God may not tell you every reason why you need to make a change, but I promise you, if you will seek His peace, He'll speak to you clearly enough for you to know He was the One who placed the order for the change.

I know a sister who took three years to heal and recover after a professional athlete, whom she dated and loved for three years prior, whisked her off to Las Vegas, married her, and 24 hours later decided he had made a mistake and wanted an annulment. A few months later he married somebody he had just met. If she had sought the peace of God, He would have told her what everybody praying for her already knew. She was blessed to be the "ex" of somebody who was godless and crazy! That change was not meant to devastate her. It was meant to deliver her!

We can't look at hard times as isolated incidents that happen in a vacuum anymore than we can see blessings as occurrences that are meant only for us. We get blessed so we can bless other people and ultimately serve the Kingdom. We get hurt, go through trials, and face heartache for the same reason. We've got to throw out those "me-colored glasses" and start seeing with the eyes God gave us.

If I am operating during a "winter" season in my life, I don't panic and worry because there's a sudden drop in my income or my ministry seems to be stalled. I trust the Lord to make a way for me and the people I'm responsible for until I make my way to my "spring." If your purpose on this earth is to preach, don't be surprised when you lose that high-paying job you've been holding onto so tightly. If you're in a preparation season, then wait, study, and pray. Because when you pass from there into your time of public ministry, you want to be approved unto God, and you may not have the abundance of time to study later that you have right now.

I've seen women who want to be married so badly that their season of singleness was spent whining and complaining about being single. They didn't use that time to serve the Lord without distraction and establish His presence in them. So when Mr. Right came along, they married him—and carried all their carnal, unsanctified attitudes and habits into the marriage. Now they're fighting to "leave" all that stuff so they can get on with the business of "cleaving." But that's hard when you haven't learned how to submit, follow, or serve.

Women and men of God, let me say this to you. There is a purpose for everything, even singleness. Don't waste your bachelor and bachelorette days looking forward to wedded bliss. If you do, your married days will be anything but blissful. Single people have time to spend hours praying and studying the Word. Married people don't. Single people can drop everything and fly halfway across the world on a missions trip that will change their lives. Married people can't. Single people can fellowship till the wee hours of the morning. Take it from me, married people have curfews. Singleness is a blessing that you should not waste. Use your singleness to let God define, then refine you so that you won't go looking for somebody else to tell you who you are or what you're worth.

131

"To every thing there is a season, and a time to every purpose under the heaven" (Eccles. 3:1). A life of order is lived as closely to ordained purpose, time, and season as possible.

Out of Order

If God is a God of order, then it stands to reason that there is a path that leads away from order. And every act that resists order takes us further along this road. *Confusion* is the destination of people determined to walk the path contrary to the will of God. Confusion, in contrast to order, is the state of things not being placed in their proper place, and therefore are unsettled. God tells us that He is not the author of confusion. When there is confusion in your life, He's on record letting you know that He did not put it there. (Guess who did?)

The way of confusion is the way of the flesh. Paul gives us two choices in Galatians 5. We either walk by the Spirit or we walk by the flesh. The flesh is that part of us that is not spirit. It is our body and our basest desires to please it.

Our spirit and our flesh war within us. Now, it seems unreasonable that God would allow such a war to take place. We can't get away from our flesh; we have to take care of it, feed it, wash it, exercise it, and give it rest. So how do we do that and fight with it too?

The key to winning the war with the flesh is in understanding two things. First, God's order provides for our flesh. We are expected to do all we can to keep ourselves healthy so that we can do the work of the Kingdom, enjoy our spouses, procreate, fellowship, and care for others. But the flesh has a natural craving for sinful things, and order dictates that we make the choice not to give in to those cravings. Secondly, that same Spirit that discerns godly things, gives us the desire, the ability, and the energy to do godly things.

That said, how many of you know that we don't always want to listen to the Spirit, much less follow His leading? That's where confusion comes in. Remember our discussion about sin in the last chapter? Every act of disobedience takes you further from God and gives you more options for more disobedience. It's like following a road that forks into two or three more roads every few hundred yards or so. The more you follow it, the harder it is to figure out which direction you came from and whether or not you're anywhere near where you planned to go when you started out.

The components of purpose, time, and season are still in effect when we walk according to the flesh. But without order there are some startling and frightening differences. Without order, there is no reason for anything. When you take God out of the equation, you have eliminated everything except what isn't God. So that leaves you without light, truth, hope, justice, holiness, power, life, and the Spirit. What's left? Darkness, lies, hopelessness, wickedness, cruelty, weakness, death, and the flesh.

Notice that without God, there is no life. So then everything that happens moves you closer and closer to death. (Well, Romans 6:23 does say that the wages of sin are death.) So purpose, time, and season without order also take us toward death. Purpose without order becomes simple conduct. Time without order becomes a ticking clock. And season without order is reduced to circumstance. And these three work, not always in concert, to move us progressively toward confusion and ultimately death.

So if change for the man or woman walking in the Spirit is purpose, time, and season acting upon us, around us, and between us to serve God's established order, to meet His ultimate goal to love us fully and be loved fully by us forever, then:

Change without God is conduct, the clock, and circumstances acting upon, around, and between man to serve confusion, whose ultimate goal is to fully consume us (bring us to our complete end).

When change enters a life that is lived out of the will of God, it is not welcome. Why? Because the flesh is fighting to live, and change without God moves us toward death. Even though all flesh must eventually die, our flesh, without the truth of God, will lie to the very end and fight anything that threatens to expose the lie. But let's think for a minute about just how confused our flesh is. If we gave our flesh all the food it asked for, we would eventually die. Yet, it has a natural tendency toward gluttony. Our flesh desires to be rich, but it doesn't desire to save or invest; just spend. Our flesh wants to live forever, but it rejects all the things of God, the only source of life.

To the man or woman who doesn't know God (and to some who do), change looks like a monkey wrench thrown into the works. You see, without the order of God, man has to try to create his own order, then control it. Without God, we don't have personal value, love, companionship, peace, joy, wisdom, hope, or true wealth. When you walk in the flesh, you have to manufacture all these things, then try to keep track of them.

That's why self-help peddlers take in billions of dollars every year from godless folks looking for hope and wisdom. That's why cosmetics companies, clothes designers, and plastic surgeons are raking in record revenues. People are looking for their self-worth in fake faces, fake hair, fake boobs, and fake status through designer labels and expensive cars. That's why Internet dating, pornography usage, and homosexuality are so accepted. People are trying to manufacture love, companionship, and joy without God-ordained order.

Every change in the life of confusion makes that person more and more afraid of losing control. So then every reaction to change is a feeble attempt to regain some of the control that was lost. When we walk in the Spirit, we don't have to keep track; we just have to follow. The road is there—just one road—and we already know where it is going to end: with eternal life. We know the truth that this mortal body of ours will die. We don't have to fight to keep it alive. We know that our days were numbered before we got here. We know that there are no urges that control us. We know that there is nothing anyone or anything can do to destroy us until God is ready for us to go. We do not have to live in fear, because we have faith; and with faith, we have hope.

Reason to Celebrate

All the time we spend here on earth is to change us. Our very desire to know God is a desire to change, because to see Him is to change. All

134

God's plans for us require change, or we would be living them already. He promises us success and prosperity. At what? Change and find out. When? Change and find out. Will you have all you desire? Change and find out. How good can life get for you? Change and find out.

When we yield ourselves to change, we gain access to untold treasures. We discover the most precious thing in the world to God. We find ourselves. Jesus said that he who would lose his life would find it (see Mt. 16:25). When we abandon the destructive desires of our flesh to resist change and embrace the order of God, we find out what Paul found out. Our bodies are a temporary dwelling place housing a spirit anxious to behold and experience life in unrestricted communion with the Father. We find out our purpose here and trust the Holy Spirit to empower us to fulfill it. We begin to see the glory of God in everything, and by that we are changed daily into His image.

And soon, God willing, we will not be able to change without celebrating...and we will not celebrate without changing!

Beloved, now are we the sons of God, and it doth not yet appear what we shall be: but we know that, when He shall appear, we shall be like Him; for we shall see Him as He is (1 John 3:2).

Praise God for change. Jesus changed His majesty to manhood to come to earth as our ransom. And as we daily walk with Him, we will discover, from glory to glory, just why we mean so much to Him.

Change Your Mind

Do you realize that before He made the world, God knew the things that would give you joy and decided to shift the entire universe to make sure you would have access to them? Did you know that He is concerned about every tear you cry and wants to hold you every time you're afraid? Can you imagine being loved by Someone who has everything, knows everything, can do anything? And can you imagine Him loving you so much that He would give it all up just for you?

I know that we say we're saved, but really take some time and think about what that means. Don't think, "He *saved* me," or "He saved *me*." For as long as you can, meditate on the statement, "*He* saved me."

1. Think about the last big change in your life. Now list every different event, person, moment, and decision that was in any way a part of the change.

2. Now list every Scripture that you can think of that was illustrated in that change or in the process of embracing it.

3. What are some of the reasons you believe God put you on this earth?

4. What season do you believe you're in right now, and why?

5. Spend time looking at a tree, a body of water, and a building. How much, if at all, do they remind you of God or His ways? If you can't think of anything, take a moment to pray and ask God to show you what He would have you see.

"Once upon a time there was a man named Andrew Carnegie who lived in New Jersey with his two daughters Aneicka and Andrea, and he traveled to California to meet the woman named Wanda Ann who lived in California with her two daughters Wendy and Whitney and their husbands Steven and Timothy and one grandson Steven Wayne..."

CELEBRATE!

Chapter Eight

Party Time!

Lift up your heads, O ye gates; and be ye lift up, ye everlasting doors; and the King of glory shall come in. Who is this King of glory? The Lord strong and mighty, the Lord mighty in battle.

—Psalm 24:7-8

"God cannot endure that unfestive, mirthless attitude of ours in which we eat our bread in sorrow, with pretentious, busy haste, or even with shame. Through our daily meals He is calling us to rejoice, to keep holiday in the midst of our working day."

—Dietrich Bonhoeffer

Since the beginning of time, God's created human beings have struggled with change. But why? Were we not created in the very image of God—the same God whose very words changed nothing with something, then gave something form and form light, then light night, and night day? Isn't He the same God who painted the earth with sea, land, and sky, then declared that they would retain, sustain, and be changed by all life and living creatures forever?

From the moment "Let there be" left God's mouth, "be" began to change, and it has not stopped changing from then to now. In fact, it is changing even as you read this. So why do we—whose very souls are inflated with His breath—not live in joyful anticipation of change? Nothing that encounters God remains the same. Do we not know that change is our only evidence that God is with us?

You have been cordially invited to a celebration of change. God has been planning this party for some time, even before the world was set on its foundation. He's just waiting for you to give Him a date. Check your calendar. Is today good for you? I know you're going through a storm right now, and you're thinking you'd like to hold off on the party until weather permits. But you should know that God doesn't have to ask permission from storms. In fact, that storm you're in had to ask permission from God before it blew into your life. And God allowed it, because the truth is He loves throwing parties in inclement weather. The more windy, cold, and rainy it is, the better.

In Mark 4:35-41 we see that Jesus planned a little change celebration on a boat. The Word says the storm was so bad that the wind blew the water into the ship until it was full. The disciples were about to sink. And where was Jesus? He was taking a little nap. Scripture says He was "asleep on a pillow." The verb tense indicates that He had been that way for a while.

Can you relate to that scene? Is the storm you're facing right now so bad that you can't see any way out of it, and Jesus seems to be off somewhere getting some shut-eye? Jesus knew the storm was coming. Why did He take you out to sea, too far out to swim back to shore and nowhere near a lighthouse or a safe harbor? Doesn't He care?

Mark 4:38 says the disciples woke Jesus and said, in effect, "Don't you care that we're about to die in this storm?" Did you notice that nobody asked Him to stop the storm? That's because they didn't imagine that He was that awesome. They just woke Him up because they wanted Him to join them in their fear. What are you asking Jesus for? Are you just asking Him to cry with you, validate your fear, or feed your anger or uncertainty?

Nowhere in Scripture does it say that Jesus answered their question...with words. And why should He? It was a ridiculous question. It didn't deserve an answer. Still, He was gracious enough to prove His love with actions. Don't waste your time asking Jesus to tell you He loves you. If you're not certain, ask Him to prove it.

Jesus got up, and Mark says that He rebuked the storm. As a matter of fact, Mark, Matthew, and Luke use the same word. That word *rebuke* means to evaluate. Look at Jesus. He got up in the face of that storm and just told it what it really was. And what He said was, "Peace, be still." In the Greek, "peace" means "an involuntary stillness, or inability to speak."[1] *Involuntary.* The storm didn't want to stop being a storm, but Jesus evaluated it and said, "That's enough. You've got these people thinking they're going to die because of you, but I'm on this boat. That means Life is on this boat. Now shut up!" To "be still" means to be muzzled. I love my Lord. He made the storm unable to speak, then put a muzzle on what was already being said. Now that's power.

The Word says there was a great calm after Jesus spoke. That literally means there was a mighty, loud, large, exceedingly great...quiet. Deafening silence from the storm that had so much to say just moments before. And when all was quiet, and Jesus had rebuked them for their lack of faith, the disciples wondered amongst themselves, "What manner of man is this, that even the wind and the sea obey Him?" In that storm, the disciples were changed. They found out that calling on Jesus didn't just mean they'd have somebody to hold their hands when they were scared. They learned that calling on Jesus meant they didn't have to be afraid. Wasn't that change worth the storm?

What about you? Do you realize that the storm you face is talking loud and saying nothing? Your Lord and Savior has already evaluated the storm. He has already told it that it cannot continue to speak fear into you and that whatever it is already saying is silenced. And the minute you believe Him, you'll receive one of the greatest gifts of your relationship

---

1.   Spiros Zodhiates, *New Testament Word Study Book* (AMG, International, Inc., n.d.).

with Christ. You'll get to experience the "quiet storm." It's one of the perks of your salvation contract.

Circumstances may not change right away, but you do. You trade your fear for faith, your panic for peace, and your disheartenment for hope, and every demon that plagues you will be obliterated in battle as the whole force of the heavenly army comes to your defense. Now, what did you say about not wanting to have a party in a storm? Jesus changed the disciples in the storm so He could do mighty things with them on the other side of it. Right after the storm, demons were cast out, a ruler's daughter was brought back to life, and a woman who had an issue of blood for 12 years was healed. Now that's a celebration!

The party is not all the dancing and shouting you do when you come through the storm. The party is the unleashing of the power God wrought in you through the storm. The disciples were given power over unclean spirits after that experience. There is so much power, ability, and direction that God wants to give you, but He needs to change you so you'll have the faith to receive it. If you are changed by the knowledge, through experience, that Jesus can "evaluate" a thing and change its behavior, and that His power is your power, you won't hesitate to believe that you can speak to issues in your life and in the lives of others. Child of God, the storm is your engraved invitation to a roof-raising, praise party *par excellence.*

All Dressed Up

When we celebrate change, we declare that change is a reason for celebration. Change, then, is the garment we wear to every occasion. Surely you didn't think that no one would see your change. No one lights a candle and then hides it from view. God didn't put that light in you so you could hide it from others. Men will see your change, delight in it, and glorify your Father in Heaven.

Change comes in a lot of different styles, and we have to make sure we're wearing the right garment for the right occasion. But all of them are made from the pattern of truth found in the Word of God. That's because our Divine Designer wants to put His mark on everyone who wears one of His garments. A good designer makes clothes that look good. A great designer makes clothes that look good *on*. When you see a change in somebody's life, you know right away if it was a change made by God, because it'll look like it was made just for them. You can recognize a Holy Ghost original right away.

Look at that woman. She was supposed to be married last year, and it didn't happen. But she looks so peaceful. That's a Holy Ghost original. That brother's wife used to be the loudest, craziest, meanest thing. Do you know that next month they're renewing their wedding vows? It's a Holy Ghost original. He got laid off with only six months' severance pay. But two days later he found a new job, and the company he used to work for was sold and everyone there was fired. Holy Ghost original. She was 15 and pregnant. She tried to get an abortion, but her parents wouldn't let her. Today is her baby's 15th birthday. As she lights the candles on his cake, the Lord speaks to her. She is called to preach the gospel to troubled teens. Holy Ghost original.

Wear your change proudly. And when people ask you where you got your peace, how you weathered that storm, where you found the strength to survive that tragedy, when you learned to forgive that betrayal or pray for that one who abused you so, tell them you have a Personal Designer who makes every good and wonderful thing they see on you and in you. Tell them that they can find Him "in the book." He's very reasonable. In fact, His garments are free for the asking, and they always fit you perfectly. Actually, you don't have to go looking for Him; He'll find you, but make sure you open the door when He knocks. Don't keep Him outside waiting.

The Guest List

I'd rather spend an evening with five or six funny, personable, joyful, down-to-earth individuals, than sit at a Beverly Hills banquet with five or six hundred boring, pretentious, stiffnecked people. When you make a decision to celebrate change in your life, you might want to do a quick double-check of the guest list. Some people want to show up just to see if you really survived, so they can try to knock you down again or go tell folks that you're just faking. You can't be that joyous and peace-ful after what just happened to you. These are what I call "party poop-ers." Others know you're throwing a party in the midst of a storm, and they've just come to loot. They are the "crashers." Party poopers and crashers are the people you should make sure to cross off the list.

As I mentioned earlier, there was a woman who was angry when she heard of my engagement to Andrew. She said, "Why would God bless her to be married twice when some of us haven't been married once?" Party pooper. There are people who haven't spoken to you since God blessed you with that promotion and that raise. They've been telling people that you've gotten "grand" and don't care about your "real friends" since you've been hanging out on the boss' yacht and hobnobbing with all the other vice presidents at the company. But the truth is *they* can't handle your promotion because a jealous, envious spirit is taking root in their heart.

Party poopers will make you ashamed to praise God for your bless-ing. They will make you think your celebration is prideful boasting. But remember what Jesus told us to pray in the previous chapter. "Thy will be done" and "Thine is the glory." When you ask God to have His way in your life and He blesses you, you'd better not let shame steal His glory.

Another thing party poopers will do is try to keep you from having a party at all. They will see a change sitting right on your doorstep, but they'll try to discourage you from embracing it. You single mothers who have been treating your son like a surrogate husband will try to talk him out of marrying that beautiful woman who loves him because you don't want to be left alone. Let him make that change and celebrate, without guilt. And you fathers who haven't been there for most of your daugh-ter's life. Don't try to make trouble when her new stepfather wants to adopt her. Don't block her from making that change. When the time comes, she may choose a better father for her own child than her mother did if she has a father figure in her life who knows how to love her.

146

Party poopers are hard to recognize sometimes because they are usually among our friends and family. Crashers are a lot easier to spot. They're usually not invited to celebrate change with us because we know they aren't really rejoicing with us. Crashers are those people who were the most vocal in celebrating your hardship and spread the most gossip about you in your struggles. A crasher will casually drop by when God blesses you with a new house (to replace the one your ex-husband and his new girlfriend are living in) and look around. By next week, everybody in town knows how many bedrooms you have and what kind of toilet paper is hanging in your bathroom.

I don't let crashers get anywhere near me. I can spot them coming. Their mouths are full of negative words and their hands are out, palms up, ready to snatch your joy, your peace, your soda, your husband, and anything else they can get. A crasher will see a woman with a broken heart and try to take advantage of her vulnerability. A crasher will ask a man of God, who's trying to walk holy, to come over to console her, and meet him at the door wearing nothing but a T-shirt and a lame pout. Crashers want to take as much from your celebration as they can, even if it means taking the celebration itself.

When you celebrate change, celebrate with people who know you and love you or who need you. Those who know you and love you understand why you're celebrating, and they want to celebrate with you. Those who need you, who need to see how you handle change, will celebrate with you because you have given them hope and confidence that they can endure.

I encourage you to fellowship with other believers as you work through your change to celebration. You never know how much of a blessing you might be to them. And I exhort you to serve others as you see them go through changes. Serve them with understanding, wisdom, kindness, long-suffering, and support. Serve them by not judging them as Job's friends did or abandoning them like the man at the pool of Bethesda was. Serve others through their changes and through yours. Sometimes it's so easy to forget that the world is going on, even as we change. The people we love still need us to care. The people we work with still need our labor. And God still expects us to worship Him as we go through changes. Sometimes that's the only way we'll make it through them.

Who's Performing?

Nothing ruins a party like bad entertainment. It follows then that we can't call people to join us in our celebration of change and not give them something special to talk about when they leave us. The headliner at every change celebration is the one everybody came to see. And believe it or not, that person is you. I know, you're thinking, *No, people need to see Jesus.* You're not trying to steal His glory, and that's good. But part of His glory is seen in how He changes the torn-up, messed-up, wrecked lives of people like you and me.

Revelation 12:11 says that one of the things that God uses to overcome satan is the "word of [our] testimony." Our witness is one of the weapons God uses to defeat the enemy. Every time you change and others see it, and you tell them that God did it, you deal another blow to that liar, that serpent. You just learned how powerful words are in a storm; your testimony puts a muzzle on the devil and shuts up all the lies he's been telling about you.

This book is part of my personal testimony, given to you to shut satan up. And I don't want to just keep him from spreading his lies in my life. I want him to stop speaking to every man, woman, and child who has ever been afraid of change. I want you to know that shaking in your life only gets rid of the things that shouldn't have been there in the first place. There are some people who were in my life when my first husband died who are not here today. There are some people who were at my church who are gone now; ministries and traditional ways of doing things that went away when God shook the place up.

I'm here to testify that weeping is truly only for a night and joy is definitely on the way. I love my husband Andrew C. Turner with all my heart. He is not a "replacement" for Wayne Davis; he is "a new thing," and I am a new woman because he loves me. I'm living proof that you can do all things through Christ. I could not see past my grief long enough to even think about tomorrow. But by the power of His Spirit, I stand today, victorious, over sin, over sickness, over depression, over heartache, over storms, over financial difficulties, and over personal attacks and public ridicule. My testimony, child of God, is not that I am victorious over change. My testimony is that I am victorious *because* of change!

So, welcome to my party. Don't worry. You're not late. This cele-bration is going to go on forever (*literally*). Eat your fill of the word in my testimony. Drink from the rivers of joy that spring up from my heart. Dance with me, because I could always use a dance partner. Or you can just listen to the "songs of deliverance" that play loudly wherever I go (see Ps. 32:7). Socialize. I'm sure you'll see somebody you know.

Maybe you're planning a celebration of your own. I see some things are already changing for you. You've read this book. You're ready to kick up your heels, aren't you? You've been through some storms, and I also see you're wearing your custom-designed Holy Ghost party clothes. They look good on you. So when's the party? Today? Good! I hope you'll invite me. Better yet, why don't we combine our parties? The more the merrier. Besides, we do have the same guest of honor, and I'm sure He wouldn't mind. He's planning a huge party of His own right now. He's keeping most of His plans a secret, but I do know this much:

> *Let us be glad and rejoice, and give honour to Him: for the marriage of the Lamb is come, and His wife hath made herself ready. And to her was granted that she should be arrayed in fine linen, clean and white: for the fine linen is the righteous-ness of saints* (Revelation 19:7-8).

I'll see you there!

Change Your Mind

Pray this prayer with me:

"Father, in the name of Jesus, I accept Your gracious invitation to change. I recognize in my heart that You desire change in my life in order to bring me closer to You. I *do* want to be closer to You. I want to delight myself in You as You delight Yourself in me. I want to know Your will for my life. I want to experience the strength of Your joy and the transforming power of beholding You in everything I see. I believe that I can do all things through Christ, and I yield to Your desire to move in me, through me, and for me. I will wait for You to change me, according to the order You set down before You loved me in my mother's womb. I know that they that wait on You shall renew their strength. I am renewed today as I mount up on wings as eagles. I shall run and not be weary. I shall walk and not faint…for I will celebrate change. Amen."

1.   Meditate on each part of the prayer. Be blessed.